Santa Miracles

50 True Stories That Celebrate the Most
Magical Time of the Year

Brad Steiger &
Sherry Hansen Steiger

adamsmedia
Avon, Massachusetts

Published by
Adams Media, a division of F+W Media, Inc.
57 Littlefield Street, Avon, MA 02322 U.S.A.
www.adamsmedia.com and *www.cupofcomfort.com*

ISBN 10: 1-59869-612-2
ISBN 13: 978-1-59869-612-7
Printed in the United States of America.

J I H G F E D C B A

Library of Congress Cataloging-in-Publication Data
available from publisher.

Interior photo © Martin Valigursky / istockphoto.com

This publication is designed to provide accurate and authoritative information with regard to the subject matter covered. It is sold with the understanding that the publisher is not engaged in rendering legal, accounting, or other professional advice. If legal advice or other expert assistance is required, the services of a competent professional person should be sought.
—From a *Declaration of Principles* jointly adopted by a Committee of the American Bar Association and a Committee of Publishers and Associations

Many of the designations used by manufacturers and sellers to distinguish their products are claimed as trademarks. Where those designations appear in this book and Adams Media was aware of a trademark claim, the designations have been printed with initial capital letters.

While all the events and experiences recounted in this book are true and happened to real people, some of the names, dates, and places have been changed in order to protect the privacy of certain individuals.

This book is available at quantity discounts for bulk purchases.
For information, please call 1-800-289-0963.

Introduction

When our daughter Melissa was teaching English in Japan, we were surprised when she told us that Santa Claus was extremely popular in all the department stores and served the same role as the jolly iconic representative of the December holiday that he did in North America.

Apparently, Santa's popularity in Japan has not diminished in the years after Melissa returned to the States. Recently, a diver dressed as Santa Claus swam with a dolphin at Sea Paradise in Yokohoma, Kanagawa, Japan.

Nearly every city in the United States has its own Santa Claus parade, and even small rural villages have Santa arriving by fire engine or some other vehicle to greet the kids with bags of candy. There is hardly a mall or department store that doesn't have Santa and his elves visit for at least a few days during the festive season between Thanksgiving and Christmas Eve.

In 1937, Charles W. Howard established a Santa Claus School that still thrives today. Located in Midland, Michigan, the mission of the school is to uphold the traditions and preserve the history of Santa Claus.

This is not a book about who Santa Claus is, but, rather, a collection of stories about the miracles of happiness, love, and joy that his spirit can bring to individuals of all ages.

There are numerous histories of the evolution of Santa, the best-known and best-loved of all mysterious gift-givers in the world. Numerous scholars agree that there were many Pagans who worshipped a red-clad hearth god who would come down the chimney to bless those he deemed worthy of his favor.

Others have traced the origins of Santa's supernatural powers to Norse legends of Odin, who flew across the night skies and cured those who sought his powers as a god to heal them of illnesses contracted during the long winters. Some researchers suggest that traditions about Odin became combined with those of his fellow Norse god Thor, who rode a chariot drawn by two goats named Cracker and Cruncher. And some scholars claim that Santa is simply a modernized version of the tribal shaman, who dressed in brightly colored robes and who may have worn a set of antlers as a symbol of his mystical powers.

Christmas as a time to honor the birth of Jesus probably began about the year 336 when Roman Christians combined their observance of their savior's nativity with Saturnalia, the popular Pagan celebration of the festival of lights that coincided with the Winter Solstice on December 25.

To find a precise date for the advent of a Santa Claus figure in Christian Europe is more difficult. We know that the popular bishop Nicholas of Myra, who died in Lycia, Anatolia (present day Turkey) on December 6 in about 350, had a reputation as being a generous person who was even capable of producing miracles. Credited as the "Worker of Wonders" both before and after his death, Nicholas was recognized as a saint by the Eastern Catholic Church in the Eleventh century. By that time, he had become the third most beloved figure in Christendom, after Jesus and Mary. He became the patron saint of Greece and Russia, as well as many cities throughout Europe.

But the question remains: When did St. Nicholas become associated with the idea that his spirit could mysteriously visit good children on Christmas Eve—or December 6, depending upon the family's location?

We believe the tradition began in a French village on December 6 sometime during the twelfth century. Honoring their patron saint, St. Nicholas, local nuns decided to bring candy to all the children in the village who had been good during the past year. The nuns entered some homes when the families were away and left candy in the shoes of the good children and switches in those of the naughty children. Because the energetic nuns managed to cover so much territory, some parents thought it had to have been St. Nicholas himself who had brought the gifts. From this French village and the efforts of the generous nuns, the Christmas visits of St. Nick spread slowly across all of Europe.

The evolution of gifts from candy to larger items may have been a result of the blending of traditions regarding the three Magi, the three wise men from the Orient, who brought gifts to the manger where the baby Jesus lay, and the giving of gifts by the Romans who celebrated Saturnalia. The belief that St. Nicholas enters a home through its chimney survives as a tradition established by the Pagan hearth god's means of entry.

St. Nicholas was often named according to the spirit that he represented. In France, he was known as "Pere Noel" and in Spain as "Papa Noel," Father Christmas. In Denmark and Germany, his title became

"Christmas Man." In northern Germany, interestingly enough, he was named after the Christian holiday— "Christkindle" or "Kris Kringle," the latter of which has become an alternate name for Santa Claus in our contemporary culture. During the 1500s, the English dropped St. Nicholas after the nation became Protestant and favored naming the miraculous gift-giver "Father Christmas," a much thinner and austere individual in contrast to plump old St. Nick. In the 1600s, when the Dutch began immigrating to the British colonies in America, they brought with them their "Sinterklaus" or "Sinte Klaus," who, in their colony of New Amsterdam (presently New York City), became Santa Claus.

The Dutch colonists viewed Santa Claus or "Santy" as a very tall, slender, dignified, and somewhat stately individual, as befitted a benevolent saintly spirit. Washington Irving, famous for his tale of the eerie spook, the Headless Horseman in "The Legend of Sleepy Hollow," reinvented the traditional image of the somewhat aloof Santa Claus and in his *A History of New York*, recast Santy as a good-natured, jolly guardian spirit who soared above the treetops in a wagon and dropped presents down the chimneys of good children.

In 1822, Clement C. Moore wrote the classic poem, "A Visit from St. Nicholas," which described Santa

Claus driving a sleigh drawn by eight tiny reindeer. Moore also spoke of Santa as being a jolly, plump elf, thus linking him to the ancient Pagan traditions of the generous shaman surrounded by his supernatural entities, the elves, the same beings who observed humans throughout the year to see if they merited being blessed or gifted during the Yule season.

Thomas Nast, a political cartoonist, famous for popularizing the image of the Democratic Party's donkey, began in 1863 to create images of Santa Claus for the Christmas covers of *Harper's Weekly*. In 1866, inspired by Moore's poem, Nast created the famous drawing of Santa Claus in his North Pole workshop, reviewing the list of good and bad children. Santa is depicted as definitely plump and jolly, a cheery gift-giver who rides off into the night on a sleigh pulled by reindeer to deliver gifts around the world.

Nast captured the image of Santa Claus that remained virtually unchanged until slight modifications were made in 1931 in the advertisements featured on the back covers of popular magazines. Coca Cola, the popular soft drink, commissioned artist Haddon Sundblom to paint a new Santa in their print ads from 1931 to 1964. Building upon Nast's famous drawings, Sundblom polished the image of Santa Claus that is most well known today—a plump, jolly, red-cheeked, white-bearded man attired in a bright red suit trimmed with white fur, a black belt, and leather boots.

The depictions of Santa Claus in the popular media—especially, perhaps in motion pictures—remain very flexible. In the warmhearted classic, *A Miracle on 34th Street* (1947), a department store Santa might really be the kindly old elf himself. In *The Santa Clause* (1994), a man commits the unthinkable when he accidentally kills Santa and magically begins transforming into Santa Claus and assuming his duties. The 2007 film, *Fred Claus* reveals two startling bits of information: St. Nicholas has an older brother who has always been jealous of Nick's selfless acts of generosity; and once an individual is canonized, his entire family remains frozen in time. Because of Nicholas's status as a beloved saint, Fred, a ne'er-do-well still alive today, is given the chance to redeem himself by helping his brother, Santa Claus, at the North Pole. The trapped-in-time destiny of a saint's family no doubt came as news to the Vatican.

As we declared at the beginning of this Introduction, this is not a book about Santa or the many traditions that surround him. The Santa Miracles experienced by the individuals who have contacted us throughout the years really occur in a magical space and time that may well be separate from the normal three-dimensional world that we all share. Indeed, some of the miracles described in this book may have taken place within a timeless magical kingdom that contains the essence of the true meaning of Christmas.

It is our firm hope that all readers, young and old, will experience the "deep magic" and true wonder of this collection of Santa Miracles.

—Brad Steiger and Sherry Hansen Steiger

As is true of many of us, David Oester learned about Santa's miracles as a youth. This is his story:

Let me give you some background. I attended the first six years of school in a two-room building; the first room held the first through fourth grades and the second room was for the fifth and sixth graders. The schoolhouse was located at Deer Island, Oregon, a campsite used by Lewis and Clark on their journey to the Oregon coast on November 5, 1805. In the 1950s, it was a wide spot on Highway 30 that followed the Columbia River to Astoria.

It was during this time that my dad, Raleigh Oester, got a job as a rural mail carrier for the Deer Island area. These were hard times for many people. I remember one of my classmates would not come to school one day a week, and it was always the same day each week. It turns out that that particular day was washday at his home and he only had one shirt and trousers to wear.

Another friend never wore shoes during the summer, as he had to save them for the school year.

I didn't realize while growing up that an economic depression had caused severe poverty. I had food to eat and a shelter over my head and never gave it another thought. I never knew that it was hard on my mom and dad who struggled to keep us clothed and fed. Recently, my mom told me that a few days before Christmas she would hide some of our old toys and then wrap them up so we would have something under the Christmas tree to open.

My most vivid childhood memory is when my brothers and I would accompany my parents on Christmas Eve to spread some holiday cheer. Dad would put on his red Santa suit, complete with padding and a fake white beard, load up the car with presents, and deliver gifts to some of the children on his mail route who he knew would not have a Christmas because money was too tight.

I did not realize at the time that many of the homes we visited were not much more than shacks. Dad knew the names of everyone in each household.

He knew the hardships they suffered, as he too experienced them in the past. He would park the family car away from the driveway so the occupants would not recognize it as the mailman's car. Then, my dad would call out the names to my brothers, mother, and I, and we would retrieve the presents and stuff them into his white bag.

When the family answered his knock on the door, he would greet the parents and children by name. They had no idea how this man dressed in a red Santa suit and a white beard could possibly know their names. The children's eyes would shine with a brightness that is hard to explain, and the parents' mouths would drop open in shock.

I remember the last stop we made. Dad walked up to the dairy farm, passing the main house, and stopped at the hired hands' cabin. He knocked on the door, and when the children opened it, he greeted them with a "Merry Christmas" and handed out the wrapped gifts.

While Dad was delivering the presents, I asked my mom why he gave away all the presents. I was thinking of how nice they would have been for our own Christmas.

Mom looked at me and said, "Those children will not have a Christmas; their parents are too poor to buy their children anything. You will have a Christmas, and now so will they."

"But why does Dad dress up as Santa," I asked. My mother told me it was so not to embarrass the families. They must not think it is charity, but a miracle on Christmas Eve.

I never forgot the kindness that my parents showed for those who were less fortunate than we were. My dad never attended church, but he lived the higher spiritual law of "love thy fellow man," a lesson that has stuck with me.

Years later, as a husband and father, when my oldest son was working on his Eagle Scout badge, he chose a "sub-for-Santa" project. He collected newspapers and soda cans, held car washes, and created other money-making projects to raise money for a family with two children who could not afford Christmas presents.

My son bought gifts for each of the children and cooked a turkey, potatoes, and all of the other trimmings for a nice Christmas dinner. A local merchant donated a Christmas tree and he built a tree stand, wrapped the presents, and together we hauled the dinner, presents, and tree to the family's home.

When my son told the woman who answered the door what he was doing there, she was shocked—especially when she saw the tree, dinner, and gifts my son brought into the house.

Even after he set up the tree and delivered all the gifts, the family had no idea who this young man was or why he performed a miracle for them on Christmas Eve.

I was so proud of my son for carrying on the tradition begun by his grandfather.

Jacob White is completely convinced that he saw Santa Claus when he was eight-years-old. No one will ever convince him otherwise. Here is Jacob's story:

I grew up in a small town in Idaho, not terribly far from Boise City, and every Christmas the entire White family would drive to the old home place outside of Nampa where Grandma and Grandpa White still lived. Everyone—my mom and dad, my two uncles, my aunts, and us five cousins—would try to arrive two or three days before Christmas Eve. We'd attend Christmas Eve services at the little country church that my father and his two brothers had attended as kids, and then we'd head back to our grandparents' big, old farm-house for a fantastic dinner.

Grandpa White always had a Christmas tree set up in the living room, and on the first day that all of us cousins would arrive, we would have the honor of decorating the branches with the same lights, colored balls, and streamers that had served the White family for at least thirty years. I remember that some of the wires for the lights had electrician's tape wrapped around the worn spots.

On Christmas Eve, after Grandma White read "The Night Before Christmas," the kids were sent up to bed. Since it was a large house, there was plenty of room for everyone. My brother John and I got one room with a double bed, and our three cousins—Grace, Judy, and Margie—got another with two single beds. Since Grace, at eleven, was the oldest, she claimed a bed all to herself, while Judy and Margie had to snuggle up in the other bed. John and I could hear the girls whispering and giggling, and we lay there talking about what we were going to get from Santa on Christmas morning.

Grace, who thought she was so smart and grown-up, had tried to spread doubt earlier that evening when she said that she didn't believe that there really was a Santa. She got shushed pretty quickly by her parents, because she was upsetting Judy and Margie, who were both five years old and firm believers in Santa Claus.

I had heard rumors myself from some kids at school who no longer believed in Santa, but Mom said that they were certain to get lumps of coal in their stockings on Christmas morning. I didn't repeat the negative whispers to John, who, at six, had no doubts about the reality of the big guy in the bright red suit.

Grandma White had replaced the usual night light in the hallway with one shaped like an angel in honor of the season. Both the bedrooms where we cousins lay trying to fall asleep faced the hallway, and as I was lying in bed looking at the light, my eyelids grew heavier. Johnny was just drifting off. At least two of the girls were still whispering.

Suddenly, the night light was blocked by the shadow of a very big man. The adult men in the White family were all tall and quite thin. This man was extremely rotund. I shook Johnny awake, and I could hear the girls beginning to talk out loudly.

From above his head, a reddish light shone on the man. We could all clearly see the image of Santa Claus. He wore a red suit, black boots, and his white beard came down to the middle of his chest. He stood there for about ten seconds or so, smiling and waving at us. Then he disappeared.

All five of us kids ran screaming down the stairs. It was a wonder that one of us didn't trip and break a body part or two. We scampered into the living room, shouting at the top of our lungs that we had seen Santa Claus. Grace—the scoffer, the disbeliever—was screaming the loudest.

It took a long time for the adults to get us kids quieted down. We had all seen the same thing: A fat, jolly, bearded man in a bright red suit. Of course, all the grownups laughed at us. Grandpa wondered if we had sneaked down the stairs and sampled some of the cider from the big glass bowl while they weren't looking.

Since Grace and I were the oldest, we were singled out for false accusations of having told the younger kids ghost stories and having managed to scare them—and ourselves—with our spooky tales.

All of us kids knew what we had seen, and when we get together now, we still talk about the night we saw Santa Claus. It didn't matter how much our parents and Grandpa and Grandma teased us; we knew that for some unknown reason we were blessed—singled out, if you will—to have seen Santa.

I have thought long and hard about our vision over the many Christmas Eves since that very special one. Santa Claus is a supernatural being, and maybe as a spirit, he really can project his image to thousands, maybe millions, of kids who truly believe in the idea of a kind, benevolent gift bearer. Or perhaps the spirit of Christmas itself can manifest to the hearts and minds of young children however they may best receive the message of love and sharing.

Bruce Shayne Nelson told us a remarkable story of a true Santa miracle his cousin Tom had related to him that occurred during Tom's service in Vietnam:

One Christmas a few years back, we sat around the dining room table in Grandma's apartment: uncles, cousins, grandchildren, nieces and nephews, most of us stuffed with too much Christmas food and drink, listening to the shouts of the kids playing in the back room, to the voice of an uncle on the phone exchanging Christmas greetings with a relative in another state, and to the sound of the football game on TV mixed with carols from a little radio somewhere. In the air was the pleasant confusion of a late evening Christmas family gathering. Outside there was hardly any snow, but enough of a nip for it to feel *Christmassy*. Inside, we were moving to that mellow state which comes toward the end of a nice family holiday gathering.

"'I'll be Home for Christmas.' I love that song," Tom said as he toyed with a piece of pumpkin pie. "I've *always* loved it."

"Sure. It's a wonderful song." I concurred.

"For me," Tom went on, "it goes all the way back to 'Nam. That's where that song really meant something. In a jungle full of guys who wanted to kill you and in heat that had you sweating day and night."

"I'll bet." I said.

"That year, all of the guys in the outfit decided we were going to have a Midnight Mass on Christmas. I mean, guys of all religions, you understand. It was somehow just understood and agreed on. So we ordered up a chaplain."

"You *ordered* one?"

"Yeah, you know the Army," said Tom. "And it wasn't easy, either. Nothing's easy in the Army, particularly in 'Nam. Headquarters came back and said that maybe we *could* get a chaplain for Christmas Eve, but only if we had an 'appropriate space' for him. You know, such and such enclosed space, with so many places to sit, an altar, lighting . . . I forget all the details, but there were plenty. You know how the Army is."

"Sure, I guess I do."

"Well, what was really nice, I think, was the way everyone really pitched in. It was a lot of work getting that space together in time for Headquarters to approve it. And I think every guy in the outfit put in plenty of extra effort to make it happen. It was great!"

"But how did the idea get started?"

"Oh, jeez, sometime in October or something . . . I don't remember just who came up with the idea first, but before you know it, it was like *everyone's* idea. We scrounged, and swapped, and built, and dug and . . . and remember, we were doing this in the middle of a war. And in between the times we were trying to deal with Charlie. I mean, we weren't just sitting out there in the bush, we had a war going on. Like a lot of little guys hiding in the foliage a thousand yards away, or so—armed with pretty nasty weapons. Just try to level a terrain in those conditions, and then somehow come up with a hundred folding chairs or benches out in the bush like our outfit was. That stuff doesn't come in on the choppers . . . not usually."

"So you improvise."

"Yeah, or build it, or scrounge, as I said, but we were motivated. We were gonna have that Midnight Mass, period."

"And you did."

"Oh yeah, and how!"

"We even managed to cobble together a Santa costume for the big night," Tom chuckled. "You can imagine how tough that was, rounding up three or four yards of red material in the middle of a South-east Asian jungle, and getting it sewn together into something resembling the Old Fellow's traditional outfit. You won't find many tailors in a company of infantrymen . . . but we still pulled it off. The mess sergeant, affectionately known as 'Tubby,' had the right figure for the job, and he agreed to be our Saint Nick on the big evening. The suit, which two of the boys eventually stitched together, fit him surprisingly well.

"An even tougher feature of Santa was the beard. One of the lads went as far as risking his neck by heading outside the perimeter and combing some nearby villages, trying to get something that would serve as a respectable beard. He claimed he had even offered to buy the beards off several of the old Viet grandpas in the region, but without any luck.

"'It didn't matter how much I offered, those old dudes just kept shaking their heads,' he said.

"So, our two volunteer tailors finally tore the Major's pet pillow apart and somehow got that sewn into a beard that almost looked like the real thing. With the whole outfit in place, Tubby looked a heck of a lot better than he ever did in his combat fatigues.

And seeing him there, blazing red and sweating like a horse in the boiling sun of Nam, practicing his 'Ho ho ho!' we all suddenly knew the rest was going to fall into place.

"And just the space was something. We had two huge hospital tents sewn together. It was beautiful. It didn't look like any church I'd ever seen, but considering where we were, it was quite a creation."

"And the chaplain came?"

"Oh yeah, we did our part, so they finally sent in a chaplain by chopper. Just in time for Christmas Eve."

"A great moment, huh?"

"Sure, here we are a thousand miles from anywhere, having Midnight Mass, just like we were home. And we're all singing. This chaplain had a nice strong voice and he's leading us in all the Christmas songs."

"Like, 'I'll Be Home for Christmas'?"

"Lots of them. And right in the middle of singing that one, Charlie opens up and we start getting rained on. Incoming mortars."

"Wow!"

"But this chaplain was something, you know. We got us a good one. He just kind of raised his voice a bit, sang louder, you know, and kept on singing, and we all stayed there singing with him. And not just that song, either. On he goes to the next, and the next."

"And the rounds are still coming in?"

"Cripes, I'll say. But at that point, no one was going to give up, not if the chaplain didn't. Normally, you'd run for the sand-bags and the shelters, but we just went on singing. It was something."

"You were *all* crazy!"

"It was Christmas! And hey, I told you, we were decided we were gonna have that Midnight Mass."

"Hell or high water . . . or mortars."

"Exactly. And the best thing was, about the time that service was over, Charlie finally let up. Ran out of mortar shells, maybe. And we came out of the tent and the place was flattened."

"The tent?"

"No, everything *but* the tent! I'm telling you that those incoming rounds had leveled everything above ground. But not a single guy in the outfit got hurt."

"Because you were all in the tent."

"Yeah. Normally, an attack like that, you'd have at least have a couple of casualties. Even with everyone dug in. Maybe more. Like, *right* next to the chapel we had put up the mess hall. Made of corrugated iron and stuff like that. It was *flattened*, gone, like just about everything else in the camp. If we'd been in *there*, there wouldn't have been many of us left in one piece."

"But no one got a scratch!?"

"I'm telling you, we could hardly believe it ourselves. Not even any shrapnel coming through the walls. And the funny thing was, all the rest of camp had been in the pitch dark, the only thing lit up at all was our tent chapel. Lit up like the proverbial Christmas tree."

"A miracle?"

"Call it what you want. It was great!"

"I can understand a little better now why you like that song so much!"

"Yeah," said Tom, a far-away look in his eye. "It always takes me back, you know what I mean?"

"Sure, but it's twenty-five years later, Tom, and this time you are home for Christmas."

"Yeah," said Tom. "Except when I hear that song. And then I'm back in 'Nam. At the Midnight Mass of my life and a real Santa miracle."

Bill did not hesitate to admit that growing up in a medium-sized city in Arkansas, he had been a troubled teenager. He quickly added that he had never done any kind of drugs or physically harmed anyone, but he had expressed his teenaged angst in acts of vandalism against people's property. And once, he admitted, he did do something that could have resulted in someone getting badly hurt—if he hadn't been arrested before his prank went too far.

At thirteen, Bill had begun his career of minor crimes by perpetuating an age-old tradition of flushing a cherry bomb down a toilet in the boy's bathroom at Thomas Jefferson Junior High School. He had made certain that he had been alone in the bathroom before dropping the depth bomb into the toilet, so he got away with that serious prank without being caught. Unfortunately for the school's budget, the cherry bomb managed to spring severe leaks in some outdated plumbing and flooded several classrooms on the floor below.

The fact that Bill's nasty deed remained cloaked in anonymity encouraged him to continue his minor reign of terror. He consistently egged his math's teacher's car until she finally had to get a new paint job. He threw a rock through the picture window of a grocer who had caught him stealing some candy bars and who had threatened to call the police if he ever again caught Bill shoplifting.

Bill's life of crime came to an end one Halloween night, however, when at the age of seventeen, he was caught dropping ripe tomatoes on cars passing under the Twelfth Street bridge. Bill was laughing so hard as the rotten tomatoes spattered on the hoods, roofs, and windshields of unsuspecting motorists that he didn't even hear the two police officers who came up behind him and grabbed him by the arms.

"What's the matter with you, kid?" one of the officers growled. "You could cause someone to have an accident!"

"C'mon, officers," Bill laughed. "It's Halloween night. You know, trick or treat."

The shorter, stouter of the two officers shook his head and looked at Bill as if he had discovered a new species of idiot. "Well, punk, this little trick of yours is going to earn you a real treat in the slammer."

Bill was incredulous. The police officers were actually going to arrest him for such a harmless prank as dropping rotten tomatoes on cars. Unbelievable. Where was their Halloween spirit?

By the time the judge had finished lecturing Bill, he had a clearer idea of the terrible consequences that his "harmless" Halloween prank could have worked on unsuspecting motorists who suddenly had one of his tomato bombs splatter across their windshields, thus startling them, possibly blinding them, and causing them to crash or to careen into oncoming traffic.

The desk sergeant had called his parents, and Bill could hear his mother crying throughout the judge's harsh scolding.

"I felt terrible hearing Mom crying," Bill said, "but the fact that Dad was standing there so quiet and grim-faced bothered me even more. I didn't fear a whipping when I got home. Neither of my parents every laid a hand on me. But I really looked up to Dad and I knew I had disappointed him."

Bill's parents would have to pay a fine for his act of public vandalism and possible crime of reckless endangerment. He was sentenced to sixty days of community service. Bill was also ordered to return to the court on December 15.

Bill said that he put on his best "tough guy" act when some of the neighborhood boys would come by the areas where he was picking up trash in public restrooms or raking leaves in the parks. He had never before smoked cigarettes, but whenever he saw any kids he knew approaching him, he would shake one out of a pack and light up. Sometimes he would cough or his eyes would tear up from the smoke, but he always managed to have a butt dangling on his lips when his friends came around.

He took a lot of teasing about getting caught and being a punk from some of the actual tough guys in his school, but Bill had a ready lingo all set to spiel off that would put down the police and ridicule the judge. In his opinion, Bill gave the impression of the perfect social rebel, hostile and defiant against all authority figures.

On December 15, Bill stood once again before the judge and heard him pronounce his final act of community service.

"I couldn't believe my ears," Bill said. "He ordered me to put on a Santa suit and distribute gifts at the local orphanage on December 23. Two police officers—the same two who arrested me—would officially escort me to and from the place."

As he left the courtroom, Bill was handed a Santa suit, complete with cap and broad black belt. The desk sergeant, a man of at least 260 pounds, chuckled and advised Bill to tuck in lots of pillows to fill out the suit. That was the suit that he always wore when he played Santa for the department Christmas party.

Word soon got around at the high school about Bill's unusual sentence, and because at that time he weighed about 145 pounds, he was constantly teased about having to put on some weight before his debut of Santa.

"I still played the tough guy," Bill said. "I told everyone that I was going to put Tabasco sauce and red peppers in the little kids' candy, that I would put dead mice in some of the packages, that I would smoke a cigarette and try to have Santa's beard catch fire."

On the afternoon of December 23, while his mother was helping him adjust the pillows in the over-sized Santa suit, she asked Bill to treat the little orphans with kindness. Bill grunted.

"I'm serious," his mother said, her eyes misting. "Those little children are so desperate for love and affection, hoping so much that some family, someone who will be their mommy and daddy will come to the orphanage and say, 'Oh, you sweet little girl, we want you for our daughter.'"

Bill remembered being puzzled by his mother's display of emotion. Suddenly she sat down on the edge of his bed and began to cry. Bill sat down beside her and awkwardly placed an arm around her shoulders. He had never before seen his mother cry, and he felt helpless.

She wiped her eyes with a handkerchief and took a few deep breaths, trying to compose herself.

What she said next, Bill remembered, truly rocked his teenaged world. "I was an orphan," she said. "I know the pain of living with dozens of other kids, hoping the next couple through the orphanage will pick you and allow you to have a home life. I . . . I was never chosen. I never had a family life like your father and I have tried to give you."

Bill protested. She had always told him that Grandpa and Grandma Meyers had died in an automobile accident when she was a little girl and she had gone to live with her aunt Sara.

His mother nodded. Her parents had been killed in an car accident—when she was twenty months old. The administrator of the orphanage in which she lived until she was eighteen was such a kind lady that all the children called her "Aunt Sara." She had won a scholarship to college. The second year that she was teaching elementary school, she had met Bill's father and they were married soon afterward.

"I did not have any time to absorb this incredible revelation from my mother," Bill said. "She had barely completed her story when the doorbell rang, announcing the arrival of my two escorts to the orphanage." All the way to the orphanage, the two officers warned Bill to be on his best behavior. Finally, one of them turned to him in the backseat and said that he actually looked pretty good in the Santa suit.

"I had none of my usual repertoire of wisecracks with which to snap back at the officers," Bill said. "All I could think about was the terrible time that my mother had to go through as an orphan, being rejected time and time again by prospective parents. How she must have hoped this or that couple would be her mom and dad, then being left, rejected with the other little boys and girls who no one wanted. For the first time in my life, I really, really appreciated Mom. How could she be so kind, so understanding, so well-adjusted, so resourceful, after all she had been through?"

And then Bill thought of what a disappointment he must be to both his mother and his father. Here he was a troublemaker, a juvenile delinquent, almost a criminal—and they still loved him and treated him with respect. They had stood by him in court and had never once brought up his arrest or his having to do community service. They had been supportive of everything that he had ever done. How could he be such a misfit when he had such wonderful parents?

Against every ounce of his will, Bill suddenly found himself crying in shame and humiliation.

"Hey, kid, what's the matter?" the stout officer asked, looking over his shoulder.

"I have a cold," Bill said. "I have to blow my nose."

Bill dug in the pockets of the Santa suit, looking for something with which to blow his nose and wipe away his tears.

The officer sighed and handed him a couple sheets of tissue. "Santa should always be prepared for any emergency," he scolded Bill.

"Talk about being unprepared," Bill said. "I was completely unprepared for the faces of those little boys and girls at the orphanage. I guessed the oldest kid was about nine and their ages ranged all the way down to some who were barely toddlers. But every single one of them was excited at seeing Santa. I was completely unprepared for the rush of emotion that I felt when I felt their joy.

"And in every little girl's face," Bill went on, "I saw my mother's. Whenever I gave a toy to one of the girls and saw the expression of gratitude, I saw my own mother as she must have looked at that age, grateful for any small act of kindness."

Bill knows that a skinny teenager couldn't have made a very convincing Santa Claus, but he also recalls that every child there forgave his awkwardness and his lack of experience at being a jolly dispenser of gifts. When Bill had given the last gift from Santa's bag of presents, he joined the children and two of the orphanage's employees in singing a rousing chorus of "Jingle Bells."

As he walked with the police officers back to the squad car, both of the men gave him hearty slaps of approval across his back.

"You did all right in there, kid," one of the men said. "The little guys and gals really seemed to like you."

The stout officer grumbled, "We were afraid you were going to be a wise guy, but you pulled off the assignment just fine. We'll put in a good word for you with the judge. We'll tell him that you must have had a personality adjustment."

"Either that," the other officer laughed, "or we just saw a miracle take place." As he crawled into the back-seat of the cruiser, Bill agreed with the officers that a kind of miracle had occurred.

"I suppose you can say that this was my Santa miracle," Bill concluded. "And I—not to mention my parents and teachers—were pleased that the effects of the miracle have lasted ever since."

Our old friend Jerry Twedt, a former television producer and director, currently a playwright and author, shared the following account of a Christmas crisis that had to have a little help from Santa:

My wife's will power held back the tears, but her eyes betrayed her fear.

"It will come," I assured her.

She nodded. The fear remained.

The trepidation she was feeling has been experienced by anyone who has planned a large dinner party and had the main course ruined or, much worse, not available.

It was mid-afternoon on Christmas Eve, and the *lefse* had not arrived. Barbara and I were tensely awaiting the arrival of the mailman, praying that he would have the *lefse* that my parents in Iowa had sent days before.

The tradition in my Norwegian-American family was, and is, to have fish and *lefse* on Christmas Eve. On this occasion, we had invited Barbara's parents and a number of neighbors and friends to join us. However, it is difficult to have a fish and *lefse* feast without the *lefse*.

There is not a doubt that some readers are scratching their heads and asking, "What is *lefse*?" For those of you who have been deprived the exquisite experience of devouring this Norwegian delicacy, *lefse* is an unleavened bread about fifteen inches in diameter, then cut in half. Think of a large potato cake, although the hard *lefse* we make has no potatoes in it. For the meal, *lefse* is combined with cod fish. Mid-westerners often serve *lutefisk*, which is cod soaked in a weak solution of lye water and then rinsed several times in fresh water. *Lutefisk* has a very distinctive smell. If you can get by the aroma, it is quite tasty.

The fun part of our *lefse* feast is making *betas*. To make a *beta*, you place a *lefse* on your plate; pile on boiled potatoes, fish, and cranberry relish; top it all with melted butter; roll it up like a burrito; and with melted butter oozing down your wrists, enjoy a meal fit for the Gods! Well, at least the Gods who dwell in Valhalla.

Back to Christmas Eve.

"I'll never go through this again!" I said to Barb. "I'll have my parents send down a *lefse* grill, and we'll make the *lefse* ourselves."

"Absolutely," she agreed.

Time crawled by as only time can when you are awaiting something important to happen. Finally, the harried mailman walked up to the door. No doubt he was surprised to be greeted by two frantic people who asked in unison, "Are there any packages?"

"No," he answered, in a manner that said he wished never to see another package as long as he lived. "Just the mail."

He handed me some flyers, credit card offers, and three Christmas cards from people we had sent cards to but had removed us from their list, and trotted off.

No *lefse*. Tears and terror replaced the fear in Barbara's eyes. "What are we going to do?"

"I don't know," came my unhelpful reply.

We stared at each other, then Barbara's Germanic heritage surfaced. She dried her eyes and ordered, "Go to the Post Office and check the packages!"

"They won't let me do that."

"They have to!" She answered and fled into the house. I did not argue. After rounding up our two small boys, ages four and three, I drove to the post office. I knew the last thing that Barbara needed was to deal with two squabbling children.

I approached the post office and saw that the gates to the loading dock were open. Fully aware this was a restricted area, I drove in anyway. The boys and I started for the dock, expecting at any moment to hear an employee yell to get myself and my kids off the premises. No such command was given.

I reached the dock and looked up at a kindly man of about fifty. I explained my dilemma and asked if I could please look through the packages for the *lefse*. Perhaps it was my pleading look or the presence of my boys, or something much more profound, but he sighed and pointed to a wall of boxes. We both knew he was breaking the number one rule in the postal rule book: *never let a non-employee touch unsorted mail.*

I thanked him profusely, and with the boys' help, began to sort through the stacks of undelivered boxes. It was obvious that a large number of people were going to receive late Christmas presents. *This is hopeless*, I thought. *It will take hours to go through this mess.*

My four year old, Christopher, held up a package. "Here's one, Daddy." Not to be outdone, Alexander, the three year old said, "Here's another one."

"Those aren't the ones I want," I replied impatiently. "Just stand back and don't touch *anything.*"

"Can't we help?" Alexander asked.

"I wish you could," I answered. "But neither of you can read."

I could tell from the look on his face that Alexander thought the fact that he could not read was no impediment to helping, but he and Chris stepped back while I pawed through the boxes. I was about to admit failure when I spied a familiar label partially hidden by another box. In a true "eureka" moment, I threw off the upper box and saw the unmistakable handwriting of my dear mother. "I found it!"

The boys cheered, the dock employees grinned, and I drove home the happiest man in the state of Florida. I presented the *lefse* to Barb with all the joy of the wise men presenting gifts to the Christ Child. I doubt if Barbara has ever received a Christmas present as desired as that box of *lefse*.

Now, as Santa miracles go, this was of the minor variety. I am sure you can argue that finding the *lefse* was no miracle at all, just dumb luck. However, I was allowed in a restricted area and then permitted to look through unsorted mail. I dare any of you to try duplicating that feat in a major city post office on any day other than December 24. That is why I call this a Santa Miracle.

The children were waiting excitedly for Santa to make an appearance at the Children's Center in Falmouth, Cornwall, United Kingdom. Word was that Santa was arriving by helicopter directly from the North Pole.

Actually, Santa was supposed to leave from Culdrose Airport, but his helicopter flight was grounded due to some very bad weather.

When the Falmouth fire brigade heard the news, they knew that dozens of kids were going to be very disappointed when Father Christmas did not appear as scheduled. Quickly agreeing that it was their job to help *anyone* who found himself in a difficult spot, the fire brigade decided to drive to Culdrose and rescue Santa.

Family support workers at the Children's Center said that the children's faces beamed with joy when they saw a fire engine pulling up with Santa sitting in the passenger seat. Perhaps it was not the dramatic aerial arrival that had been planned, but everyone agreed that the firefighters had performed a wonderful service, greatly in keeping with the unselfish spirit of Christmas. Besides, what could be more exciting than a shiny fire engine driving up with its siren blaring, announcing the visit of Father Christmas?

There is some precedent for Santa Claus as a superhero. In 2008, a film was released entitled *Santa Claus Conquers the Martians*, and in 1983, DC Comics published a special issue of *Superman* teaming the two champions of truth, justice, and true Christmas spirit called (what else?) *Superman and Santa Claus*.

Santa Claus impersonator Dieter Thurn, was holding court for the children in Santa's Grotto in a department store in Bremen, Germany, when he noted a couple of suspicious characters hanging out near the long line of kids waiting to see Santa.

Although the two young men thought they had escaped detection by all the surveillance cameras, they had not counted on the eagle-eyes of Santa in his grotto. Thurn was astonished as the two brazen thieves went about almost nonchalantly filling their rucksacks with expensive cosmetics from the nearby counters.

First, the children were frightened when Santa Claus suddenly shouted in a very loud voice that the two men should cease and desist.

The thieves, startled that their robbery had been detected, began to run with their loot.

Santa shot up from his throne, and with amazing speed for such a large man, grabbed the two men and held them down until the police arrived.

Daniel, a six-year-old who had watched wide-eyed as Santa sprang into crime fighter mode, told a journalist that Santa was "totally cool." Not only does Santa give away presents, but he also fights crime wherever he sees it. Daniel concluded that Santa was a superhero, like Superman, only better.

Caleb Parker had been a department store Santa for over eighteen years, but the child that he will always remember was a frail little girl named Alice.

It was a bitterly cold New Hampshire day in December when Caleb noticed a thin girl with a thread bare coat several sizes too large standing in line to sit on his lap. She was about three kids from the head of the line when she fainted.

"A couple of the children against whom she fell, felt that she was trying to push ahead in line," Caleb said. "When they saw her fall to the floor, they panicked and started trying to get back to their parents for safety." At that time, the department had a first aid room with an employee in attendance.

"Evelyn, the lady on duty in the first aid room when Alice was carried in, wasn't really a trained nurse," Caleb said, "but she had taken a couple weekend courses in health and safety that were conducted two or three times a year at the community college."

There was just something about the tiny child with the dark-rimmed eyes that cried out to Caleb. "She looked the classic waif or street kid in some old black-and-white film version of a Charles Dickens novel."

When there was a lull in the line of children waiting to crawl up on Santa's lap, Caleb put up the "Santa Has to Take a Nap" sign and headed for the first aid room.

"Evelyn had taken off the girl's coat and had her lying down on the couch," Caleb said. "She had on a nearly threadbare dress of very light weight, and you could almost see her ribs through the thin dress."

Evelyn was concerned that the child was severely malnourished. "No wonder the poor thing fainted," she told Caleb. "She looks as though she hasn't had a decent meal in weeks."

Caleb told Evelyn that he was on a break and that he would watch the girl while she went to get her something to eat from the cafeteria. Caleb handed her a couple of dollars, but Evelyn pushed his hand away and said that she would cover it.

"I've got to get home, Santa," the girl said, after she had told Caleb her name. "Can I just tell you want I want for Christmas and leave? Mommy will soon be coming home, and she will be worried if I'm not there looking after Daddy."

Caleb soon learned that Alice's father had been injured in a factory accident that summer, but they were still waiting for "'surance" to start paying some of the medical bills. In the meantime, Mom had taken a job at a grocery store where she helped people carry out their bags of groceries.

When Caleb inquired if Alice weren't a little young to care for her father, she sat up straight and announced that she was nine years old, certainly old enough to take care of Daddy.

Evelyn returned with a cup of chicken noodle soup from the cafeteria. At first Alice refused, saying that she wasn't hungry. But she soon dropped the facade. Within moments, in spite of her attempts at table manners, Alice had finished the cup of soup and was admitting that it had really tasted good.

Caleb listened as Alice told Santa what she wanted for Christmas.

"The dear unselfish child's requests were all for her parents and her two younger sisters," Caleb said.

Evelyn insisted on getting a cab for Alice in spite of all her protests.

As Caleb was leaving to assume his role as the jolly Santa on his mammoth snowdrift throne, he heard Alice give her full name and address to Evelyn. She was Alice Doyle, she said, and precisely gave her street address.

Caleb stopped in the doorway. "Would your father's name be Brian?" he asked.

Alice's eyes opened widely. "Yes, Santa. How did you know?"

Caleb smiled. "Because he was a good little boy."

Caleb had gone through all twelve years of school with Brian Doyle. At one time, they were the best of friends. They had lost touch after high school, but Caleb well remembered the times the tough Irish kid had kept him from taking a beating at the hands of bullies. He also knew that Brian Doyle was filled with pride.

After he had finished work that afternoon, he got the Doyle's address from Evelyn and told her what he planned to do.

"She helped me pick out the right size for a new winter coat for Alice and she made an intelligent guess for her two sisters," Caleb said. "On the way home, I stopped at a supermarket and loaded up with groceries. Quietly, I pulled my Pontiac up in front of the Doyle residence and put everything on the doorstep. I rang the doorbell, then ran for the car."

Caleb was just getting in behind the wheel when little Alice opened the door and saw all the packages of gifts and food. Then she got a good look at Caleb.

"Fortunately, I still had my Santa suit on," Caleb said. "Ho, ho, ho," he shouted in his best Santa voice. "Merry Christmas!"

As he drove away, he could hear Alice's voice excitedly calling to her family inside that Santa had just left something on their doorstep.

"I was not a well-paid executive," Caleb said, concluding his story," but I put fifty dollars in an envelope to Brian, with a note that read, 'You were always a good little boy. Take good care of your family and your very special daughter. Love, Santa.'"

Ed Lewis declared that he was still embarrassed to admit that he had only donned a Santa suit and visited The Good Servant nursing home because he lost a coin toss.

"I am ashamed to admit it," Ed says, "but I had an aversion to being around the elderly."

Ed had been extremely close to his maternal grandmother and when she became ill prior to her death, Ed had a difficult time dealing with the reality of aging.

"Nanna had been so full of life, so vivacious, so active," Ed recalled. "She took me to concerts in the park, to theater performances, and to the zoo. She had always been tireless, always ready to go on to the next attraction wherever it might be. She was youthful in appearance until she was in her mid-70s. Then it was if she became this little old lady overnight."

Nanna had enough money from her investments and her husband's life insurance to be able to afford a nurse to look in on her once a day. Ed will always remember the sound of her rasping cough, the smells of disinfectant, and a strong eucalyptus odor coming from the vaporizer.

"I was nineteen, a college student, a supposed grownup, and I had to psych myself up to hold my dear grandmother's hand when I came to visit her," Ed said. "I felt ashamed of myself, but I simply could not come to terms with the fact that this husk of a woman lying on the bed was really my dear Nanna. I offered thanks to God when Nanna passed, convinced that He had sent her a blessing so that she did not have to suffer the trials of growing old any longer than necessary."

Only once in the seven years since Nanna had died had Ed entered a nursing home. His wife's aunt Joyce had been placed in the Good Servant home, and Alexis insisted that she come along on a Sunday afternoon to bring Joyce some flowers.

"I was doing okay as we walked down the hallway to Aunt Joyce's room, until I caught the scent of various medicines, antiseptics, and other odors I did not attempt to identify," Ed said. "By the time we entered

Joyce's room, I could only stay long enough to wish her well and hand her the flowers. Then I had to excuse myself to find a restroom."

Ed never went back to Aunt Joyce's room that afternoon. He waited in the car until Alexis ended her visit. The angry look on his wife's face gave him advanced warning that all the way home he would receive a very pointed lecture on his rudeness to Aunt Joyce.

And so it was that on that December day, Ed looked at the back of his hand and saw that the quarter had landed heads-up. He had flipped with another member of the Junior Chamber of Commerce to see who would visit the Good Servant nursing home in the disguise of Santa Claus. Ed had called tails. There was no way out of it. He must don the Santa suit and spend an evening with several dozen elderly men and women.

The dinner hour at Good Servant was 5:30 to 7:00 P.M., so the administrators asked Ed to be there as soon after seven as possible. Some of the residents would already be getting sleepy and ready for bed.

Some of his fellow J-Cs helped him load his SUV with a bag of gifts for Ed to distribute. They had been informed there were fifty-six residents at the home, so Ed hoped that the committee had wrapped enough presents for everyone. There was a candy cane and a small plastic Santa figure in each package.

When Ed arrived at the home around 7:10, he was met at the front door by the administrator, a stout, pleasant man in his mid-fifties. He welcomed Santa to the Good Servant and rang a small bell to announce Santa's arrival.

"They're all waiting for you in the great room," the man smiled. "And they are all very excited for Santa to arrive with his sack of presents."

Ed's first impulse was to ask if the man was putting him on. How could a bunch of men and women in their seventies, eighties, and nineties be thrilled by the appearance of guy in a fake beard, a red suit stuffed with pillows, and a bag of meaningless gifts?

Ed received his answer when he stepped into the great room and was greeted by a rousing cheer from the residents and the staff members in attendance. Many of the residents were confined to wheelchairs, but a number of those who were not came forward on canes and walkers to accompany Santa as he walked toward the front of the room where a brightly decorated Christmas tree stood beside a piano. Upon a signal from the administrator, a nurse began playing, "Santa Claus Is Coming to Town."

"I could hear some of the men and women singing along with the piano," Ed said. "Nearly everyone in the room was either singing or laughing. Some were twirling around and dancing. And some were crying."

Ed admitted that those elderly men and women who were crying really got to him. "I suddenly felt like crying along with them," he said. "These were fathers and mothers, brothers and sisters—and they all had their memories of Christmases past. They all had their own precious memories of gathering with their families around Christmas trees in their own homes, surrounded by their children and parents, brothers and sisters. They were once vigorous men and women who worked hard, raised their families, and stood beside the hospital beds as their parents, their spouses, perhaps even their children, passed on to the other side. They were farmers, teachers, bankers, lawyers, factory work-ers, retail merchants—the complete width and breadth of community life. Some had been heroes, serving their nation. Others served by keeping the country running and the home lights burning. They were people!"

When he began to hand out the packages, Ed felt a strange warmth come over him. "Some people laugh when I say this, but I felt like something inside me suddenly started to glow," Ed said. "I think I had some kind of transformation experience or an epiphany of some sort."

Ed found himself laughing along with the resi-dents as he began to hand out the packages. "I did a couple of Santa chuckles, some really deep-throated ho-ho-ho's."

The bag was soon nearly empty. "I had four packages left," he recalled. "We had been told by the administrator that there were fifty-six residents at Good Servant. I thought that maybe we had packed a few extra, and I was about to hand them to some of the nurses when one little lady came up to me and said that some friends of hers were too weak and sick to come out to the great room. She asked if Santa would please come to their rooms and give them their gifts."

Ed experienced a few unpleasant memories of the sick room that Nanna had occupied until her death and the manner in which he had rudely excused himself from Aunt Joyce's room. For a few moments the odors common to rooms in which old age and illness are claiming the vitality and life of once active and completely functional humans came back to cause him a few moments of hesitation.

Then, with a hearty Santa chortle, Ed said in a booming voice, "Lead me to the rooms of those boys and girls."

The lady who so cared about her friends took Ed by the hand and began to lead him down the hallway. A number of elderly men and women in their wheelchairs formed a train of laughing and giggling participants in the surprises that the residents forced to stay in their rooms were about to receive.

"I'll never forget one woman and the way that she smiled and whispered a 'thank you" when I gave her a brightly wrapped gift," Ed said. "Even then, as she lay on her pillow, her white hair billowing out around her head, I could tell that she had once been a beautiful woman. I held one of her hands until a nurse stepped into her room and told me that she had had enough excitement for one night."

As Ed drove home that night in the Santa suit, he said he spotted a shooting star streak across the cold December sky. He jokingly told himself that that was Santa's sleigh out for a trial run before the big night.

"I felt really good about myself for the first time in a long time," Ed concluded his story. "Before I had left the Good Servant nursing home that night, I told the administrator that he could count on my being Santa again next year."

Gary will always remember the miracle that Santa performed for him when he was in third grade.

"When I was a little kid, I had a real problem with my weight," Gary said. "I know the pain of being called "Fatty, Fatty, two-by-four," "Tubby," and "Fatso" on the playground during recess. And walking the five blocks home from school every day nearly always meant being teased. Kids would grab my lunch pail and pretend to find steaks, roasts, mashed potatoes, or whole pigs inside."

Gary said that nearly every night after school he would go up to his room and lie on his bed and cry. His older brother Ray was no comfort. He would listen outside the door and wonder aloud who the little girl was who was crying like a sissy in his room.

Ray was thirteen, much taller than Gary thought that he would ever be, and stout of build, but not fat. Gary's parents were a bit on the heavy side. His dad would sometimes comment that Mom was "pleasingly plump." Gary deemed himself to be disgustingly fat, doomed forever to be an object of ridicule and mockery.

Ever since first grade when Christmas rolled around and the teachers began to plan the holiday program for the parents, Gary was selected to play Santa Claus.

"I know the teachers thought that giving me the starring role would build my self-confidence," Gary said, "but I know that I was chosen because I was fat. The trouble was, I really had to work hard to act jolly like Santa, because my little heart was breaking inside that Santa suit."

"Although the third grade class was coupled with the fourth grade for the Christmas program and there were a lot of boys taller than I was, none were plumper, so once again I was fat old Santa," Gary recalled. "I felt it was my destiny to be Santa until I graduated from high school—and then probably the only career open to me would be as some department store Santa."

When he was in the third grade, Gary said that he was a firm believer in Santa, but he was not so true a believer that he accepted every fake-bearded guy in a red suit to be the real McCoy.

"One afternoon after school I made my way to a local department store that featured a Santa Claus," Gary said. "I wasn't going to tell him what I wanted for Christmas, but I was going to ask him for some advice."

The area of the department store that housed Santa's workshop was very nicely done. There were a number of animated elves tapping away with little hammers at a variety of toys. A large Christmas tree with beautiful decorations and lights stretched above the display, and Santa sat on a massive chair behind an icicle-covered arch to suggest the cold of the North Pole. Mrs. Santa Claus, a rather imposing woman with a large mane of snow white hair, stood outside the arch, limiting Santa's visitors to one at a time.

Gary stood in line, waiting his turn, summoning his courage. When, after what seemed hours, it was his turn to crawl up on Santa's lap, he nearly cried when Kris Kringle smiled through his fake beard and observed, "My, you're a heavy little boy, aren't you?"

After the traditional "ho-ho-ho" and the "what do you want for Christmas, little boy" had been uttered, Gary whispered that he hadn't come there to declare his wish for any presents.

Puzzled, Santa frowned, and attempting to maintain his jolly demeanor, asked Gary "Why, then, have you stood in line for so long? Why did you come to Santa's workshop?"

Feeling his face turning a fiery red of embarrassment, Gary said that he knew that the man wasn't the real Santa.

When Santa protested that, indeed, he was, Gary said, "I know that the real Santa is busy working with the elves making presents at the North Pole. But what I want to know is, why does Santa have to be so fat? Why do I have to be so fat? Every year at Christmas, I have to play Santa Claus at school. Do you have to be fat to be Santa?"

It all flowed out in a torrent of painful words of frustration and hurt.

"Don't you wonder why you are so fat, Mr. Pretend Santa?" Gary went on. "Doesn't it bother you to have people call you Fatty, just so you can be Santa at Christmas time?"

Santa sat in silence for a moment, and Mrs. Claus reminded him that other little boys and girls were waiting to tell him what they wanted for Christmas.

Just then, Gary started to cry. He tried so hard not to, but the hot tears stung his eyes, and he couldn't help himself.

"Kid, don't cry," Santa said in a voice very different from the jolly old elf, "look here, look here."

The man was pulling aside his suit and showing Gary the pillows and stuffing under the suit. "I'm not fat," he whispered. "I ain't skinny, but I ain't fat. It's not being fat that makes a Santa. I really love kids, and I really love this job, and I really like making kids feel good about maybe getting what they want for Christmas."

The man smiled and winked at Gary. "Look, the rest of the year I work on the loading dock of the store. All the guys know the way I love Christmas—the whole magilla: Santa, the elves, Rudolph, and the reindeer. So when the guy who used to play Santa got too old and cranky, the manager came to me and said, 'Murphy, you're the new Santa. We need someone playing Santa who loves Christmas and kids.'

"You just gotta fill yourself with love for life and other people," Murphy said, giving Gary's hand a squeeze. "You don't have to be fat. You don't have to be skinny. You just gotta be you. And never be afraid to be you."

Gary nodded his understanding, thanked Santa, and slid off his lap.

"Maybe I didn't really understand everything the man had said right at that minute," Gary said, "but the more I thought about what he said, the better I felt about myself."

That night at the elementary school's Christmas program, he was the absolute best Santa that he could be. "I gave an Academy Award-winning performance," Gary recalled fondly. "I gave it my all. My parents were proud; my teachers were complimentary; and even some of my harshest detractors gave me a couple 'good job, Fats.'"

Inspired by the pride he felt the night of the Christmas show, Gary cut down on snacks and junk food. He talked Ray into working out with him. When his father saw Gary's sudden interest in athletics, he bought the boys two sets of dumbbells.

At Christmastime in fourth grade, the teachers decided that Gary should play the part of one of three Wise Men who traveled to the manger of the Baby Jesus.

"Please," Gary pleaded, "I want to be Santa again this year, just like I have been every year."

Gary could tell by the look in the teachers' eyes that they were considering another boy, perhaps a bit heavier for the role.

"Just one more year," Gary said, stating his case. "I don't mean to brag, but you know what a great job I did last year. And believe me, a couple of pillows under the suit, and I'll be an even better Santa this year. I love being Santa."

Gary got the role for one more year, and everyone agreed that he had delivered another stellar performance as Santa. He was particularly pleased because he knew that he had won the role because of his ability, rather than his waist measurements.

"When it was time to cast for the Christmas program in fifth grade, I had lost so much weight that I gladly surrendered the role to another boy," Gary said, concluding his story. "However, I really hadn't grown much taller than when I was in third grade, so that year I played one of Santa's elves. I gave the audience the best elf that I could, and the boy who played Santa—who had wanted part so badly the year before—delivered a fantastic performance as St. Nick."

Until she was eleven-years-old, Julie carried a photo taken on the night that Santa Claus visited her when she was three. Whenever any schoolmate or friend would express doubt about Santa's existence, Julie would whip the wrinkled, crinkled photograph out of her purse and silence all the doubters.

"See for yourselves," she would challenge any who questioned the existence of Santa. "He came right into our house with a bag of gifts, and he held me on his lap so Mom could take a picture of us."

Triumphantly, she would smile at the "ooohs" and "aaahs" and "wows" of the once skeptical friends who now readily conceded all doubts in the face of absolute proof.

As an adult, Julie admits with a smile that she probably believed in Santa a bit longer than some of her friends because of that wonderful photograph. She also accepts the true identity of that particular Santa who visited her when her family lived in a suburb of Chicago.

"My dad had a Jewish actor friend who was big and stout and had a deep voice," she explained. "Steve loved to dress up like Santa and visit the homes of his Christian friends on Christmas Eve. He had purchased a very nice, authentic Santa suit, and as an actor, he really knew how to apply the false beard so it looked absolutely real. He also applied just enough makeup so his rosy cheeks looked like he had stepped off a sleigh that had come from the North Pole."

Although Julie had met Steve before, he was completely unrecognizable when he came through the front door on Christmas Eve. "Of course my mind was completely blown to see Santa coming into our home with a big sack of presents for my older sister, my two brothers, and me. He was Santa to perfection.I have never seen a department store Santa that could come anywhere near his magnificent presentation."

Julie remembered that she was in her long white nightgown and holding a new doll in the picture that she carried for so many years.

"It was our custom to open some gifts on Christmas Eve, then hang up our stockings for Santa to fill during the night while we slept," she said. "There hadn't been many gifts under the tree that year. Dad later admitted that things were tight financially, and we had the joy of each other. I was perfectly willing to accept that, but now I understand that he had wanted Santa's bag to be full of gifts for each of us kids. But I did have a new doll, just like the one I wanted."

Julie laughs now that she nearly squeezed the stuffing out of the doll when Santa arrived.

"And when he picked me up and held me on his lap, I knew it was the real Santa," she said. "Mom and Dad had taken me to see the Santa at Marshall Fields in downtown Chicago, and even I knew with the discerning eye of a three-year-old that he was not the real Santa. Based on my previous Santa encounter, I could speak for years with great authority that there, sitting in Dad's easy chair in our living room, was the real Santa."

Santa held little Julie in his lap all the time he was handing out gifts to the children. When all the presents were given out, he put a gloved hand to his ear and said that Rudolph was calling him back to the sleigh. "I have to move on to visit the homes of other good boys and girls."

With a hearty "ho-ho-ho, Merry Christmas, and good night," Santa walked out the door. But never out of Julie's sacred memories of that night.

Julie has always kept the photo of that glorious occasion. "My daughters are still young enough to accept it as awesome proof that Santa is real and that their mother was once chosen to meet the true Santa Claus."

When Ruth Butler's husband died, her nine-year-old son Kenneth was devastated. Her daughter, Janice, who was four, seemed unable to grasp fully the concept of death. She knew her father had been ill for quite some time and she kept asking when he would be coming home from the hospital.

"Ethan passed in November, shortly before Thanksgiving," Ruth told us. "I tried to divert Kenny's thoughts toward Christmas and Santa, but those words sounded meaningless and hollow to a nine-year-old who had just lost his beloved father. I became quite upset when I received word from his teacher that he had become disruptive in class when the children were given an assignment to write their letters to Santa. He had disturbed a number of his classmates when he had shouted that all he wanted was his father to come back to life and Santa couldn't do that."

Before his passing due to lymphatic cancer Ethan, Ruth, and their children spent as much of their remaining hours together as possible. Masking his pain with a broad grin, Ethan helped make his coming transition less traumatic for Kenny and Janice.

"In retrospect, we probably kept too much from Kenny, who was old enough to understand some of what was happening to his father," Ruth said. "Ethan tried to continue playing catch with Kenny and carrying Janice around on his back just as long as he could. Finally, he became too weak to play with the kids, but he continued to read them bedtime stories.

"One night as he sat in his easy chair reading to the children, his voice suddenly became no more than a rasping whisper," Ruth said. "He set the book aside, put his arms around the children, and asked me to come nearer. He told us all that he would always love us, then he smiled and closed his eyes."

The children thought that their father had fallen asleep while reading to them. Ruth held back her tears long enough to call an ambulance. Ethan never regained consciousness and died early the next morning.

Kenny had been very close to his father. He had always been an exceptionally healthy boy, very athletic and sports-minded, but now, after Ethan's death, it was all he could do to nibble at his food. He seemed to lose all interest in school, and he seldom bothered to return the telephone calls of his friends or respond to their invitation to come outside and play football. Kenny would sit for hours in front of the television set, but he wasn't really watching it. Although he had scarcely wept or shown any outward sign of grief, it was apparent that he had been devastated by his father's death.

"Ethan had always made a big deal out of Christmas," Ruth told us. "He had grown up in Minnesota, and although he missed the big snow banks and the white Christmases, he decorated the house with Santas and angels and set up his prized models of what he called his Christmas Village, miniatures of an old English village at Yule. This year, Kenny wanted nothing to do with any of it."

Ruth did buy a small artificial Christmas tree in spite of Kenny's indifference toward continuing his father's elaborate celebration of the coming of Santa and the onset of the holidays. Little Janice helped her mother decorate the tree and clapped her hands in glee when the lights were turned on.

Although Ethan had absolutely no culinary talents and freely admitted to his friends that he could barely boil water, he loved to make popcorn for the kids on special nights when the family would all watch a movie together. On Christmas Eve, he performed the ritual of making a special bowl of popcorn for Santa. Ethan made up stories of how Santa's favorite snack on his rounds of delivering gifts was to nibble on popcorn. Bah! Humbug to cookies and milk! Santa craved popcorn.

On Christmas Eve, Ruth tried her best to break through Kenny's wall of silence and sorrow by reminding him that it was time to make Santa's special bowl of popcorn. Kenny shook his head at his mother's suggestion. "Only Dad could make the Santa popcorn," he said. "Remember, he had the special recipe that his family had passed on for generations. Only Dad could make it."

At that very moment, little Janice lifted her head and sniffed the air above her. "Mmmm," she smiled. "I smell popcorn!"

Startled, Kenny inhaled the fragrant aroma of freshly popped and buttered popcorn. "Mom!" he shouted, wide-eyed with wonder at the miracle. "It's Daddy's special Santa popcorn for Santa's bowl. Smell it, Mommy! That's Daddy's famous popcorn, the family recipe."

"We all smelled it," Ruth said. "The aroma of freshly buttered popcorn was coming from the kitchen and filling the entire house. It was the unmistakable scent of Ethan's special popcorn for Santa Claus's snack. We all breathed its glorious smell as deeply as we could."

The aroma of popcorn lasted for about three or four minutes, then it was gone as quickly as it had come.

Kenny's eyes filled with tears. "Daddy wants us to make popcorn for Santa, doesn't he?" he asked his mother. "I used to watch Daddy real close. I think I can remember the special recipe."

Janice squealed her excitement. "We're going to make popcorn for Santa, just the way that Daddy did."

The memory of that wonderful contact with the loving spirit of Ethan Butler will stay with Ruth and her children until the day that they each, in their own time, rejoin him. In his own special way, Ethan had given them a communication that they could all share and understand—and he had allowed the Light of Santa to find a place in his children's hearts that would never dim.

When Robert Miller was teaching social studies and serving as wrestling coach at a medium-sized high school back in his home town in Connecticut, he was leaving a restaurant rather late at night when he saw some teenagers hassling a street person." Robert said, "so my wife was out of town visiting her sister in Ankeny," so rather than fixing something to eat at home, I decided just to grab a bite downtown after wrestling practice was finished. Now it seemed that I was at the right place at the right time."

Robert said that he recognized one of the four kids pushing the old man around, and he shouted at the gang to stop and to go home.

The teenagers started advancing menacingly toward Robert, but the student from the high school where Robert taught recognized him as a teacher. "Hey, that's that Mr. Miller, the wrestling coach," he warned the others in a hoarse whisper. "Let's get out of here."

One of the gang shouted a profanity at Robert, then asked him if he really wanted to take up for street trash. "These bums just make a mess in the alleys and stink up the neighborhood," said the bully, puffing his chest out to fill the jacket that denoted his gang's colors. "We're just going to teach this old creep not to loiter in the streets. Loitering is a crime, don't you know that, teach?"

Angered, Robert shot back at the boys. "He has a hard enough time surviving in this cold without you guys hassling him. Leave him alone. He's a human being. Maybe some day you could end up alone and homeless in the streets just like him."

Two of the boys cursed Robert for insulting them, calling them bums.

Another of the young tough guys grumbled that the four of them could take Robert, but the kid from his high school grabbed the arm of one of the more aggressive gang members and raised his voice: "Hey, you jerks! He knows who I am. Let's get out of here right now." Robert walked quickly to the poor man's side. He had fallen to the ground and Robert helped him to his feet.

"He didn't seem to be hurt too badly, but as I was helping him to his feet, one of the hoods jumped on my back," Robert said.

For someone who had wrestled all four years of high school, made the team in college, and now coached wrestling, it was a simple move for Robert to flip the kid over his back and toss him on the street.

"I told you idiots that he was the wrestling coach," Robert overheard as the rest of the gang helped their fallen warrior to his feet. Within the next few seconds, they were all running away.

The old man thanked Robert for coming to his rescue. "I'm not a street person," he said, brushing snow and mud off his coat. "I'm not homeless, and I am not a bum. I'm just old."

Robert insisted on taking the man inside the restaurant for a cup of hot coffee. At first, the man protested, but he at last allowed Robert to take him by the arm and lead him into the warmth of the restaurant.

"He was really quite a good-sized fellow when I saw him up close and he was leaning on me," Robert said. "He had a rather long beard, but he was nearly bald on top, and we had to find his stocking cap to cover his head before he would leave the street."

After he had taken a few sips of coffee, he extended his hand and introduced himself as Nicholas Christian. After Nicholas had warmed up, he became quite talkative, explaining that he had retired some years ago, and, after his wife had died, he rented a small apartment that suited his Social Security budget. His son had been killed in Vietnam, but he had a married daughter who lived in New Hampshire.

"It was when he was talking about the pleasure that he took in visiting with his daughter and grandchildren that his eyes seemed to light up, to twinkle, so to speak, and I recognized him," Robert said.

Placing an arm on the man's shoulders, Robert whispered so the counter waitress could not hear him, "You're Santa Claus."

Nicholas laughed heartily, and Robert said that the "ho-ho-ho" echoed clearly in his memory.

"Yes, I used to be," Nicholas admitted. "For 28 years I was the Santa at Chandler's department store. Loved every minute of it, too."

Robert shook his head in wonder and amusement. He must have sat on this man's lap and told him what he wanted for Christmas a dozen times.

"If I had known your name was actually Nicholas, it would have blown my young mind," Robert told him.

Nicholas chuckled a deep, Santa chuckle. "Yes, and Nicholas Christian is my real name. I thought of changing it to 'Nicholas Christmas,' but I figured my birth name was close enough."

After a hearty swallow of his coffee, Nicholas asked how Robert had recognized him after all these years. After all, he wasn't wearing his red Santa suit and cap.

"It was your eyes," Robert told him. "When you were talking about your grandchildren, you had that same old Santa twinkle in your eyes."

Those same twinkling eyes were now glistening with tears. "I really miss being Santa," Nicholas said, lowering his head. "When I was nearing seventy, the managers said that I was too old. They wanted a younger Santa."

Robert laughed at the irony. All the stories about Santa Claus claimed that he was hundreds of years old, but the managers wanted a younger appearing Santa than Nicholas to listen to the children's Christmas requests.

Robert suddenly had an idea. "Do you still have the red suit and hat?"

"In my closet," Nicholas said. "I couldn't bear to part with it."

Right then and there, Robert decided that Nicholas should play Santa as a guest at the school staff party.

"The rest of the staff was totally delighted," Robert said, "and Nicholas loved being Santa again and hearing what all the teachers wanted for Christmas. A couple of the more petite women even sat on Santa's lap! A number of my colleagues even recognized Nicholas from sitting on his lap at Chandler's department store.

"I was glad that Nicholas Christian got to be Santa one more time. I tried to keep in touch with him, but I heard that he left town to live with his daughter. Just before the Christmas holiday, she wrote to let me know that her father had died in September, but that his eyes had always twinkled when he remembered being Santa at our staff Christmas party."

Ilona Szabo wrote to tell us that growing up Jewish in a devoutly Catholic country like Hungary was not easy. But Santa Claus helped her through one particularly difficult time.

Here is Ilona Szabo's story:

I was only five. I had just arrived at our neighborhood park when Peter, who was seven, ordered me away. He said no one in our usual group would play with me because I had "killed Christ."

I had no idea what he was talking about, and I doubt he had a perfect sense of his words, given his age. I did realize he referred to some terrible event, and it seemed like I was being held personally responsible. When he insisted that I had to leave, I ran home in tears.

The clarity with which I still remember the painful incident is at least partially based on my relationship with this little boy, Peter. He was my first "boyfriend," a handsome child I loved with all my five-year-old heart. Our families lived in the same Budapest apartment building, a large 1920s house by the park from which he had banished me.

So that day, quickly reaching home, I recounted my sad tale to my grandmother who was essentially bringing me up since my mother worked. Grandma Ella was a small woman—everyone in my family is vertically challenged, including me. She was not quite five feet tall but with greater courage and a stiffer spine than almost anyone I've ever known; she had escaped from concentration camp during World War II. Now she sat me in her lap, the best place I knew, hugging me while repeating in a soft whisper: "Those naughty, naughty children; nobody listens to them." Then, in her characteristically practical fashion, she began to help erase the pain by having me prepare for a much happier occasion, the arrival of Santa Claus.

Santa comes to Hungarian children on the morning of December 6. Basically he looks like Santa in America, fat and jolly, wearing a red suit and red hat, traveling from the North Pole on a sled drawn by reindeer. He is the cheery personage everyone here knows from Christmas Day. And he brings lovely presents to good Hungarian children regardless of creed. He is an ecumenical figure, good to everyone. If you were well-behaved during the past twelve months, you could expect wonderful gifts even if you were Jewish. On the other hand, if you'd been naughty . . . well, more on that later in this story. The point is that hopes were fulfilled by behavior and never by religion.

Preparations for the big event began the day before, on December 5—as it happened, the day of my painful encounter in the park with Peter. In Hungary, the period of Advent, the four weeks before Christmas itself, is filled with both church services and superstitions. Shops carried branches of fruit trees for girls in their late teens and twenties; the branches were put into water and carefully tended until Christmas Eve. If they blossomed, it meant the girl would marry during the following year.

Children followed different beliefs. Regardless of religion, the first thing you had to do was clean and polish your best pair of shoes; I did mine twice to make sure of an extra shine. Then, as custom decreed, I carefully placed the footwear before our largest window so Santa wouldn't miss my shoes while his sled, laden with gifts, circled Budapest. Tradition called for the gifts to be put right by the shoes. And Santa knew exactly what to leave because a list of goodies was always put inside one of the pair of shoes. My grandma helped as holiday tradition called for this to be in writing. She knew my heart's desires; I had found it practical to share these in the weeks before Santa Day.

Basically, I wanted books. I had learned to read, to a degree anyway. And of course my grandmother often read to me. I can't recall the exact titles on that year's Santa list but they likely included classics: Hungarian translations of *Babar the Elephant, Polyanna, Tom Sawyer, Little Women, Pinocchio, The Wizard of Oz*. Of course I also wanted more dolls to add to an already humungous collection; a person could never have enough. And I yearned for yet another teddy bear—that would make three.

It wasn't easy to sleep that night. I ran to my shoes bright and early on the morning of December 6 thrilled to discover that Santa had done his job. He delivered everything on my list, all the books and toys I wanted.

The books were especially welcome! When it came to reading, this is what I learned very early on. Reading took you away from all sorts of misery; you could become lost in marvelous stories. While you read, you could be (you were) transported to other, better worlds. Even before I was five, Santa had made all these wonderful escapes possible.

And something else: Hungarian children who had misbehaved during the previous year could expect to find birch—a bunch of branches, usually painted gold but still useful for spanking—along with regular gifts. Of course even if you'd been a little monster, you would probably not be physically punished by loving parents. But the wooden sticks were there as reminders of what might happen as a result of misdeeds.

No stick for me. Didn't my grandmother always say I was a terrific little girl? Mind you, I had never doubted Santa's wisdom regarding such important matters. But now he fulfilled my deepest need for reassurance. Obviously, I didn't kill anyone. What relief! Who cared about Peter?

But on the morning of December 6 he returned to my life. Peter arrived at our apartment with his mother, looking spiffy, even if grim.

Now, I want to say that Peter's Mom was an exceptionally nice woman, a genuinely kind soul. Grandma Ella used to talk about how good she was during the war, how she shopped for Jews in places where they were forbidden to go. I'd been in her home for dinner where she was careful never to serve pork. She knew we were not particularly religious, my grandmother did not keep kosher. But she seemed to feel she was honoring Jewish tradition by cooking chicken or fish for me. Given their past relationship, Ella felt free to confide in her friend about what had happened to me in the park. And so this woman, a truly righteous Christian, brought her son to apologize to me, which he did with seemingly genuine regret.

But the romance was over. I never spoke to him again. And I never returned to the group of children who had stood silently by while Peter so cruelly barred me from their midst. I had books and new dolls, including yet another teddy, for loving company. And I had Grandma Ella—along with Santa Claus.

J ack Velayas, an actor friend of ours, remembers the Christmas Eve when the defroster was on high, yet the rear windows of the Oldsmobile were still fogged over, as his father, mother, and he drove to his brother Ron's house.

"I was seventeen years old that Christmas and looking forward to seeing my oldest brother, his wife, and my four-year-old nephew Shawn. I sat in the back seat as my father drove with my mother by his side. Fresh in our memory was the fall of Hanoi, the President resigning in disgrace, the stock market turning bearish, and unemployment rising higher than it had since the Great Depression. The world was a very uncertain place, and there were very few reasons to celebrate. Still it was

Christmas, and we had a sack of toys in the trunk of the car for Shawn, fully aware that a four- year-old does not care about the problems of the world."

As the Velayas family pulled into the driveway of Jack's brother's farm, a cold dense fog thickened making it hard to see more than 50 yards in any direction.

"As my father shut off the car, my mother and I opened our doors, Ron's voice could be heard as he welcomed us to his place," Jack said. "As he walked up the drive to where we had parked, we could see that Shawn was with him, following excitedly as a son does, wanting to be part of any happening around the home."

As soon as the greetings were over, Jack's father turned to Ron and asked him in his most concerned voice, "What's wrong with your neighbors?

"What do you mean, Dad?" Ron asked.

Shawn looked up at his grandpa, sensing his concern.

"Well we almost hit one of them as we drove in."

"You what?" Ron asked in mock alarm.

"Yeah," Grandpa Velayas said, "and just what is that old guy doing riding around in a sleigh pulled by deer?"

By now, Jack said, his brother knew what joke his father was pulling. Shawn's eyes opened wide as he took in all the adult talk about Grandpa almost hitting a man on a sleigh being pulled by deer.

Grandpa continued on about the foolish old man. "He was just sitting there in the middle of the road in a sleigh looking at a map. I think he must have been lost or something. We almost hit him!"

Shawn let out a little gasp.

"Who is that guy?" Grandpa asked. In a very serious tone Shawn answered, "Santa Claus."

"You know, I bet you're right," Grandpa agreed. We honked at him to get him to move out of the way. And he got all flustered and cracked his whip and those deer took off. You know with all this fog we couldn't see real good, but it looked like he might have flown away."

"You didn't scare him away did you?" Shawn asked, terrified by the very thought that Grandpa, Grandma, and Uncle Jack may have frightened away Santa before he had had a chance to deliver his toys to the little boy at the Velayas' residence.

"Well, he did leave in a big hurry," Grandpa said. "In fact, he was in such a hurry that a bag fell out of the back of his sleigh. He didn't even come back to pick it up."

"Where's the bag?" Shawn asked.

"We picked it up and tossed it in the trunk," Grandpa said, barely able to contain his laughter at Shawn's concern over Santa having left without leaving any toys for him.

Shawn hurried to the back of the car and watched as Grandpa opened the trunk. There he found the bag that Santa had dropped, filled with toys for Shawn.

"That was thirty-two years ago," Jack said. "Since then my father has passed away, and I have remained close with my nephew. Today, Shawn is married with two daughters of his own, ages four and five.

"Last Christmas, I made the drive to Sacramento where they live. It was a cold and foggy night, typical for the central valley of California in winter, the evening I pulled up in front of the house."

Shawn opened the door, flanked by Bridget and Bevin, his daughters, and welcomed him into his home. Jack immediately began to tell his nephew and grandnieces about the wild neighbor in the sleigh he had almost hit with his car.

Jack turned to the girls, "I wonder who it was."

They looked up and said in very serious tone, "Santa Claus."

"You know, I think you might be right. I hope he isn't too mad at me for honking at him to get out of the way."

"You honked at him?" Bridget asked, concerned that Uncle Jack had blown their chances for any presents from Santa Claus.

"Yeah, he got all flustered and flew off," Jack told the girls. "He didn't even stop to pick up the sack that fell out of his sleigh."

At just the right moment, Jack pulled the situation out of deep despair into joy and relief. "But I picked up the bag and put it in my trunk. Shall we go see what's in it?"

"It was a magical moment of continuity between the generations. Passing the story on to my grandnieces not only added to the miracle of their Christmas, but also to my nephew's, as he recalled the story from his own childhood. The miracle of Santa is the way he adds a touch of magic to the lives of children and to adults in different ways at the same time."

Clarisa Bernhardt, who has always been deeply interested in the mystical aspects of our culture, also has a deep fascination with the concept and image of Saint Nicholas.

"Once when I was a young girl of about eight-years-old, I was looking out at the night sky, and something that resembled a cloud moved into my view. The cloud opened up, and there was Saint Nicholas."

Clarisa said that the image of Saint Nick resembled a drawing that she had seen in a book at school. But some aspects of him were quite different.

"I recognized him mostly because of his snow-white beard," she said. "It was great fun to see him in that moment and to have a glimpse into another somewhere.

He was dressed in deep-red silken robes that had many sparkling jewels scattered over his costume. These jewels may have been snow crystals that shone in the radiance of his jolly light."

Clarisa remembered that Santa appeared to be moving quickly across a field of green flowing grass and that she could see mountains in the background.

"There were no mountains around where I was living on the North Texas plains," Clarisa emphasized.

"I was thrilled to see this remarkable vision of St. Nicolas, but it was only for a moment—and then he was gone. And so was the cloud."

Eight-year-old Clarisa continued to look up at the stars that had suddenly become more brilliant and dazzling.

"I have always remembered that moment, so I have no doubt that Saint Nicholas definitely exists, even if on a higher level of awareness."

Mary Benninghoff's Santa Miracle, occurred one Christmas Eve—just when she had given up on anything good coming from that year.

Mary explained her story to us in these words:

The year 2006 was a rough year for me. It seemed that from the first day of the bright new year, I was in trouble. Early January brought a serious eye infection that threatened the vision in my right eye. The treatment went well but it was long and my eye was in pain.

My one consolation was my three cats, Cookie, Sammy, and Grady. Cookie and Sammy were adopted from Pet Refuge in Mishawaka, Indiana, where I've volunteered for years. Grady came to me as a two-week-old bottle feeder kitten and by the time he reached five months, Grady kept eleven-year-old Cookie, and Sammy, five, on their toes. Sammy adored Grady and practically raised him when he became old enough to run around.

Grady was the first kitten I raised from a baby for Pet Refuge, a no-kill animal sanctuary in Mishawaka, Indiana. I'd volunteered in the office for about three years when I jokingly said one day at the shelter, "Gee, I think I'd like to raise a baby kitten." A few weeks later, I got a call from our President, Sandy, who said, "Mary, I've got something for you."

That something was a beautiful blue-eyed, long-haired kitten who weighed about 6 ounces and was all of 6 inches long. All the way home with the baby in a tub beside me, equipped with bottles, formula, towels, heating disc, and hurried instructions, I kept repeating to myself that I was a great-grandmother. I couldn't do this! On the other hand, I kept telling myself that I had always welcomed a challenge.

Grady and Sammy played all the time as matronly Cookie watched from her high perch. They raced, rolled, and then laid down to sleep together. They were so active and most of the time, Sammy was the one to wear out Grady.

One morning in 2006 (after my eye had healed), I called the kids for breakfast, and they didn't come as usual. I found Grady and Cookie in the bedroom sitting next to Sammy. He had gone to sleep and didn't wake up that morning.

The vet said Sammy had a heart defect from birth that had never been found in his exams because it would have taken an ultrasound machine to detect it. She could not believe he lived to be five years old with a valve that was almost totally closed. His heart finally gave out.

Again, 2006 had taken from me. My cats, now Cookie and Grady, were my salvation. Through the month of March, I functioned, but I felt so guilty about Sammy. It was my fault for letting him play so hard with Grady. It was silly, of course. I didn't know about his heart, but it was my way of grieving.

We survived March, and I thought maybe the rest of the year would be better. It wasn't.

In April, I was diagnosed with breast cancer. In June, my doctor removed my breast. By taking the breast, it took all the cancer and all my reports came back clean.

I had decided a long time ago that I would be very hesitant to undergo chemo as I had friends who had passed away from complications related to the treatment. I made my feelings clear to the doctor before the surgery. Fortunately, it wasn't necessary.

As the days passed and I felt better and better, I took in a young mother cat and two kittens, six weeks old. I named them Clarissa, Chloe, and Cleo. Clarissa, the mother, was only seven months old and had had her babies at five-and-a-half months old. The kittens were adopted, but Clarissa fit in so well with Cookie and Grady, she stayed with us.

I had a full house again, and things felt normal. Soon I took in a nine-day old kitten, a bottle-feeder, I named Grayci. She was about six weeks old and I was beginning to feel that the worst was over when I was diagnosed with uterine cancer.

My son took care of Grayci when I had the surgery in October. Again, the report came back as all clear. Grayci was adopted by a great family, and I was back with my three kids.

Then, in early December, a revised report said that retesting had found a cancer cell in one of the specimen nodes they had sent to the lab after the surgery. My doctor recommended I start chemo on December 14. I told him I wouldn't even consider chemo until after the holidays, if then. I would, however, have the PET scan he had ordered.

A week before the PET scan, I received a beautiful prayer from Brad and Sherry Steiger that began, "Great Spirit." It was so moving, I said it every night (and I still do) before I went to sleep, asking that my kids remained well and safe and I be allowed to stay with them.

It was my birthday, December 22, when I had the PET scan and was told the report would take about a month. The next day, I received a call from Pet Refuge Cat Coordinator, Karen, telling me that at Cat Adoption the night before, two ladies had brought three puppies to the shelter. Two were fine, and the ladies were going to keep them, but a third little one had a severely mangled leg. She and her siblings had been abandoned, along with the mother dog who was on a chain when the owners moved out of state. Two puppies died entangled in the chain and the little one was severely injured. The vet said it was the worst case of mangling she had ever seen and with the blood loss, it was touch and go.

The puppy had her surgery on my birthday as I was having my PET scan. Karen asked if I would care for the puppy as she recovered because my home was quieter than those of most dog volunteers who fostered dogs. Naturally, I said yes.

On Christmas Eve I picked up the puppy who had been named Merry by the Pet Refuge staff. She weighed only two-and-a-half pounds at five weeks old.

I couldn't help thinking of my own surgery as I looked at her open wound. The poor thing had lost her entire right shoulder and leg.

She lay on my lap, so trusting, with the most beautiful brown eyes I'd ever seen. She whimpered a bit as I moved her from my lap to the carrier that I would take her home in. That was the last complaint I ever heard from her. She spent the night on my lap as I sat in my lounge chair and dozed. I didn't want to let go of her for fear she wouldn't be there when I awoke.

On Christmas Day, my son, Frank, picked me up to go to my grandson's for Christmas dinner. He knew I had a new baby, but his expression was priceless when he saw it was a puppy, not a kitten. I worried a bit that the day might be hard on Merry, but my daughter-in-law, Kathy, spent most of the day with Merry on her lap. As the days with Merry unfolded, and I watched her grow more and more confident, I realized that she would be as hard to give up as the kittens I raised were.

I knew I couldn't have a dog. I already had three cats, but I cried at night, thinking that I would soon have to let her go. Her wound was healing so well and soon black fuzz was covering parts of it. She didn't realize she was supposed to have four legs so the loss never bothered her as she bounced all our over our home, playing with my cats and their toys.

When she was eight weeks old, I knew the Dog Coordinator would soon want to place her with a dog volunteer, so she could become accustomed to other dogs. Then my son, Frank, called to ask if he could take Merry home for a few days to see how she would work out with their cat. I knew my prayers for her were answered. I received permission from Pet Refuge and Frank picked Merry up that day.

Merry never came back to me. Frank and Kathy adopted Merry when she was about ten weeks old. I often think Merry was sent in answer to the prayer that Brad and Sherry had sent to me. She and I healed together, both physically and spiritually. She showed a bravery and strength that made me realize how fortunate I was and as her wound closed and grew over with fur, my own wounds healed.

Merry's future was insured—and sometime after the new year began, mine looked brighter, too. The PET scan showed no cancer and I was pronounced clear.

I know now that Merry was truly a Santa Miracle. My son brings Merry over almost every week. She has grown into a beautiful fifty pound Shepherd/Chow mix with a noble Shepherd head, shiny black fur, and a gorgeous Chow tail curved over her back. Just looking at her makes me smile. She hasn't forgotten her Grandma or her first real home and she still likes to play with our cat toys. The cats aren't too sure about playing with her now that she's gotten so big.

A happy note is that Pet Refuge also rescued Merry's mother, Josie, from Animal Control where she had been taken and found her a forever home, too.

I realize now that nothing has ever made me feel more complete than raising animals. Grady was only the start to the journey. Grady is now a 22-pound Russian Blue cat and still beautiful, and I have continued to raise kittens; more than fifty to date.

It was truly a Santa Miracle when he brought Merry to us and closed a year filled with sadness and pain—but also a year that, on Christmas Eve, brought great joy to my entire family.

J anice Gray Kolb, the author of such inspirational books as *Cherishing—Poetry for Pilgrims Journeying On*, recalled that in her memories of her childhood she esteemed Santa Claus as if he were like a gentle grandfather:

Year after year as a child, the magic of Christmas delighted my heart and my entire being. I truly felt that Christmas was another realm that brought softness and tenderness and love into my life, and it seemed to be protected and surrounded by mysteries. For a short period of time, it was almost as if I was encased in a delicate snow globe with my family, and nothing hurtful could touch us. I had many wonderful days when I felt loved, but Christmas somehow was always especially magical. I have happy memories of childhood Christmases, the lovely gifts of dolls and stuffed animals that I yearned for—and my exciting belief in Santa. I have all these wonderful memories of the holidays that I shared with Mother and Dad.

Christmas will always represent love and joy to me. Going to our fine Methodist Church not far from our row home on the outskirts of Philadelphia, being comforted by the precious story of the birth of Jesus, singing Christmas carols, and placing the little figures of the Nativity scene beneath our Christmas tree are all dear memories that have lived within me through all the years to the present. And also, this little girl, who still lives within me, believes in Santa Claus.

Jesus brought such spiritual joy and Santa such happiness and love, that they did not conflict in my young life.

Along with the Nativity scene, I also displayed a jovial figure of Santa that had been given to me by my parents.

Shortly before the war years of World War II, a family moved into the end house of our row of homes. We lived in the third house from the corner with one home between us.

The new family consisted of loving parents and six children, four of them older and grown up. There were four sons and two daughters, and one girl was my age. Her name was Eleanor, the same as our President Franklin Delano Roosevelt's wife's name. We soon became friends, and I grew to care deeply about her family.

It was so amazing to me to see such a large family in the same size row home that I lived in with only my parents and a little cat. I had joy there with Eleanor's family in their home. I had never known what it was like to have older brothers.

And, oh, how they all seemed to enjoy Christmas and appreciate Santa, as well as being faithful Christians and attending the Catholic Church two blocks from our homes. Though their spiritual lives were at the center of their existence, my friend also had a strong attachment to Santa. It was beyond what I had.

I surely believed in and loved Santa's mythical image in my growing up years. I was a true believer! But Eleanor's belief was stronger than anyone else I had ever known.

Santa appeared to be such an important part of her life year-round, and she was never discouraged from thinking differently by her parents or family members. I was in her home so often, and she was permitted to revere Santa as a symbol of goodness very much in keeping with their Christian beliefs. It seemed to me that this devotion to Santa was out of the ordinary. As we grew a little older, Eleanor's belief in Santa never waned and she was often teased by our other friends.

Even though some logical doubt about Santa was creeping into my beliefs, I could never mock Eleanor. I admired her strength in the face of the teasing she often took. I wanted to retain those beliefs, too, because Christmas with Jesus and Santa was the happiest and most blessed and normal time in the life of my family. So I tried to cling to the belief in Santa, and having Eleanor as my friend helped me to be stronger in this. I just never spoke of about Santa freely to other friends unless directly questioned. But I stood with Eleanor. I never let her down.

The war happened, and slowly one by one, her three older brothers went into the U. S. Armed Forces in three separate branches. They were really nice young men and handsome and fun loving and truly devoted to their family. All were still single.

The gray air raid box now situated on the side stone wall of Eleanor's end home on the block of row homes reminded us always of the war. She and I and other young friends often sat on this box side by side, telling happy stories and trying to deny why the box was there.

The air raid box was placed under Eleanor's windows and by her side basement door, filled with equipment to be used by Air Raid Wardens when the sirens went off in the times of suspected planes approaching. Perhaps we felt that by keeping the equipment intact it would some how keep the war away. Sadly, we did not keep the war from Eleanor's family. Soon one by one, all three of Eleanor's wonderful brothers were killed in the line of duty, fighting for their country.

I have tears even as I write this, for I remember so clearly hearing the tragic news about each of these sweet guys, Bill, Bob and Al. One by one, we all saw another gold star added to the service flag that hung in their front window. First the stars were in blue, declaring that three young men served their country. Then the blue stars became gold, signifying that they had been killed in action.

It was so overwhelmingly sad and crushing to my parents and others in our neighborhood. I remember the impact of it on me to this day when I realized that I would never see and talk with her brothers again. They were my friends!

I was not familiar personally with death in those years of my young life. Eleanor's family was depleted emotionally and physically, but amazingly strong, their personal faith in Christ and their love for each other the center of their lives.

But Santa remained in Eleanor's life too. He was like a gentle Grandfather, a man who looked over her and cared about her and her family. He was good Saint Nicholas, one of the loving saints of the Christian church, and she needed him.

Eleanor and her family moved away several years after her three brothers were killed. She did not move so far that we could not visit each other at times. But eventually we parted forever, and I do not know where she and her family settled.

Wherever they are, they carry within them their three sons. And Santa! Somehow I have always believed Santa remained strongly in Eleanor's life.

I never knew a teenager who protected a belief in Santa Claus as she did. Her undeniable belief in him, despite taunting, showed me her inner strength. Could it be that the simple joyful unrelenting friendship with Santa in her personal life even in the face of ridicule, was the clue to her strength in her unbearable loss?

Yes, she and her family were all one in God, but the joys of childhood too are often gifts given us by God for strength to carry on. Perhaps Santa was Eleanor's special gift, and, in turn, she provided strength to each of her family members, a sweet bond of love from an earlier, happier time in their lives.

People, animals, legends, and beliefs from our child-hood, as well as our religious backgrounds are often carried within us in never ending ways. Sometimes they are simply necessary, and there is no other explanation. I truly understand.

When we first met Wanda Sue Parrott some years ago, she was a feature writer and reporter for a major Los Angeles newspaper. Since that time, she has written a number of books of prose and poetry.

Wanda sent us her memories of "The Night Superman Saved Santa."

A muffled voice disturbed my culture-shocked Christmas Eve. My twelve-year-old mind strained to see through suburban darkness, but drapes on the bedroom windows blocked Southern California's moonlight.

That can't be Santa Claus, I thought to myself. *He doesn't exist!*

The sound of sobs prickled my spine. *That's Sister. Something's wrong!*

I waited for Daddy's comforting voice to tell seven-year-old Jan, as he'd reassured me back home in the city, "You didn't hear monsters here. You heard the house settling."

A waterpipe banged, but the hall floor didn't creak. Daddy wasn't coming. I panicked.

The heroic figure from the comic books that Mother made me give away before our move a month earlier flashed into mind. *Save Gotham!* Superman commanded.

"What?"

Trust in me! My hero vanished.

Other nights, we were allowed to turn on lights, open doors, explore our new house. Christmas Eve was an exception. Good children stayed in bed. Bad children scared Santa away. Disobedience wasn't worth the risk of finding no stocking or gifts on Christmas morning, even though I'd guiltily borne secret knowledge a schoolmate foisted on me at Jan's age: *There's no Santa Claus. Parents give us presents.*

Suddenly I heard a *thump!* coming from Jan's room.

Something powerful seized control, forcing my hand to open my door so smoothly that the hinges didn't even squeak. I boldly tiptoed across the hall and peeked into Jan's room. Shadow light through muslin curtains revealed tangled blankets beside the bed.

"Sister?"

Jan's head poked out from the pile. "I fell out . . . I had to tinkle. I tried to hold it, but . . . now Santa won't come."

I almost laughed aloud, nearly shouted: *Santa's not real!* But another voice whispered from my mouth. "We'll fix it before Santa arrives."

Jan's whimpers stopped.

"We'll blot your bottoms dry. I'll be right back."

I crept through the living room to the newspapers stacked behind Daddy's overstuffed armchair. Our scrawny scotch pine tree was silhouetted against still-uncurtained windows, lights off. Boxes that weren't at its base earlier proved that our parents had already played Santa. *But where are the Christmas stockings?*

Impulsively, defiantly, I flipped the switch. The tree lit up, its lights miraculously manifesting magic. Through the swirl of golds, reds, greens, blues that filled the hollow in my homesick heart, I spotted two red-net stockings hanging from the knobs on our old Stromberg-Carlson console radio. Impulsively, defiantly, I snatched the stockings and, with newspapers in tow, returned to my task without turning the Christmas tree off. I hung one stocking on Jan's doorknob, the other on mine. Then I reentered Jan's room.

"Did you see Santa?" My sister handed me her damp pajamas.

"No."

I rolled the garment in classified ad pages. "Step on 'em to blot 'em."

While she kneaded the wad with her feet, I pulled linens back onto Jan's new double bed. Until our move, she'd slept in a worn out, cramped crib. Now she had a new maple bedroom set in which to grow. The mattress was damp. I spread newspapers across it, stretched Jan's sheet over them, and pressed it dry, kicking wet papers beneath the bed like I used to stash Superman comic books under mine.

"What if Santa can't find us?" Jan whispered.

"Shhhh," I said. "He's here." I opened Jan's door a crack. "Look."

The glow of lights filtered through the wall heater, illuminating the hall. The pilot light created an illusion of bustling activity. I ushered Jan to bed. "Go to sleep and don't come out till morning."

In my own bedroom I snuggled into the covers on the four-poster bed in which I was growing up. Its once-red cherry-wood spools were scarred from wads of gum I'd saved during the war, while still a tomboy who climbed trees and preferred playing animal doctor with kittens to playing house with dolls.

Before we became the first family in the subdivision carved from strawberry fields owned by Japanese-American gardeners, who'd been interned in prisoner-of-war camps in Northern California, strange things were happening to my body and mind. Boys with whom I'd played poker, kick-the-can, and baseball now caused hot flushes if we faced each other.

By the time we moved into the new house near smelly swine and dairy farms, I'd scraped, hacked, and filed the gum from the wood, and used Daddy's brown shoe polish to shine the damaged veneer, as if to give it new life.

As I drifted toward sleep, the hall floor squeaked. The toilet flushed. Then Daddy peeked in, asked if I was awake, and closed it when I didn't answer.

A loud "Merry Christmas!" startled me awake. Jan, with Mother and Daddy behind her, was standing in my doorway. "Look at what Santa gave me in my sock!"

Jan waved three Superman comics, a tube of pale pink lipstick and bottle of matching nail polish, five pairs of lace-trimmed pink rayon panties, a pack of chewing gum, and a red patent-leather wallet holding a five-dollar bill and handwritten note. "Read it." She handed me the paper.

Mother's handwritten note said, "Buy yourself something pretty to wear. Love, Santa."

Jan handed my stocking to me. "What did you get?"

Mother grimaced. Daddy grinned. And I knew that they knew that all of us but Jan knew secrets about Santa that we'd probably never discuss.

Daddy winked when I held up a jumbo Dumbo coloring book, a box of crayons, a book of paper dolls and clothes, a pink yo-yo, five tiny pairs of thick white cotton panties, a pack of chewing gum, and a one-dollar bill.

Later, when I threatened to tattle about her bed-wetting, Jan agreed to trade her stocking stuffers for mine.

That Christmas was never discussed, but every ensuing holiday, while Jan and I still lived at home, we were allowed to visit the bathroom on Christmas Eve, provided we kept our eyes shut.

Also, our stockings were hung on the correct doors with care, and we all knew exactly who had been there.

E very year Jannice Fadely tells her granddaughters this story that until now, stayed within the family.

"You can use it in your book with my permission," she said. "Many people will read your book—and they need to know the true magic of Santa Claus."

Years ago when my son Jed was about eight years old, we sat in our living room together on Christmas eve as I put the finishing details on the wooden soldiers I had made him. It was eleven thirty at night. I sat at the table, carefully painting the wooden soldiers. My son was playing quietly on the floor next to me.

We heard a heavy object land and skid to a stop on the roof of our home. We both looked up in complete surprise. It sounded like a car had landed on our roof; the thud was that loud and heavy.

We followed with our eyes the sounds of footsteps of a very large person walking up the side of the roof over the top, down to the chimney on the other side.

Completely dismayed, we both flew outdoors to see what was on our roof. There was no way for anything to land or walk on our roof—it was an A frame with a steep pitch.

The walls are 8-feet-high before you can reach the roof. There were no ladders in view. Nor were there any trees nearby. To add to the mystery, it was a very cold night, and the roof was covered in ice.

My son and I raced around the outside of the house, looking up on the roof for whatever had walked up one side of the roof and down the other. Later, we walked around the house slowly to check more carefully for something or someone on our roof.

The land around the house was completely clear of any trees or obstructions, so no one could hide anywhere on the roof. The only tracks in the snow were made by my son and me. Jed and I just stared at each other in disbelief. We shook our heads. There was no way it could have been Santa Claus.

The more we talked it over, the more convinced we were that Santa had actually landed on our roof. There was no other possible explanation.

From that night on, we both knew without a doubt that Santa Claus was real. Christmas became a very special time of year for us.

My son and I rarely tell about Santa's visit to anyone—it is just too special to share with everyone. But we tell my granddaughters the story every Christmas. It is a wonderful feeling, even at fifty-nine as I am, and thirty, as my son is, to know that Santa is real.

While some people may doubt Santa's existence, we *know* he is real.

I n these days when critically acclaimed motion pictures such as *The Dark Knight* based on the comic book characters of Batman and his nemesis The Joker are hot box office tickets and offer Academy Award winning acting, comic books have taken on a respectability that they have never before enjoyed. Therefore, we were not greatly surprised that our friend Dr. Franklin Ruehl, Ph.D, a nuclear physicist, should have as one of his Santa Miracles as a child the gift of a number of cherished comic book titles.

According to Dr. Ruehl, he experienced a "heartwarming comic book mini-Santa Miracle."

Donald Duck! Bugs Bunny! Mickey Mouse! Tom and Jerry! Sylvester and Tweety!

As a youngster, these were among my very favorite cartoon characters! I always looked forward to seeing them at the theater, far more than the movies they were paired with. Then, in the first grade, I discovered comic books which featured these very same characters, and I was immediately hooked! I would buy as many as I could afford on my tiny allowance.

Of course, in those days, comic books were only a dime apiece, so I could purchase several at a time! I never tired of reading and re-reading the episodes within.

My very favorite was "Walt Disney's Comics and Stories," which typically began with a Donald Duck feature along with his nephews, Huey, Dewey, and Louie, and often included Daisy Duck, Uncle Scrooge McDuck, and Gander Goose, followed by a Mickey Mouse entry along with Pluto and Minnie Mouse.

While in the second grade, I became seriously ill right after Halloween with what appeared to be an unrelenting cold or even possibly influenza.

My mother speculated that I might have caught a bug from staying out late on a particularly nippy evening trick-or-treating, as was my wont. I would go out until my first bag was filled, return home, then go out again for a second and even a third trip. My dad advanced the idea that I might have contracted an illness from some item that I had collected.

Whatever the cause, I began missing significant time from school which I had never done before. Extreme respiratory symptoms were plaguing me day and night.

My birthday, November 8, was ruined as well as Thanksgiving. And I was missing out on buying my beloved comic books. I was suffering both physiologically and psychologically

Two different physicians had simply prescribed the standard therapy of rest, aspirin, and chicken soup, asserting that I would recover in a brief amount of time. But, if anything, my condition was worsening.

Finally, a few days before Christmas, a third doctor diagnosed me with tonsillitis, declaring that it was one of the worst cases he had ever seen. I went into a hospital shortly thereafter for a tonsillectomy and immediately improved physically.

But I was still anguished over the time that I had lost from school, which I thoroughly enjoyed, and missing out on my cherished comic books.

A minor Santa Miracle took place on Christmas morning when I raced out to check the presents under the tree. In one large box that I opened were perhaps twenty-five comic books, including not just the ones that I had missed purchasing, but a clutch of new ones I had never seen before. My parents had been buying my favorites as well as some others as a surprise for me when I recovered. I was absolutely delighted.

For me, at that age, it was the best gift that I could have received. And that box of comic books at Christmas became a tradition for several years to come. Again, while perhaps relatively insignificant on the cosmic scale, it was very significant on my scale!

The fact that my parents would fulfill my most heartfelt wish by bringing me the comic books that I most wanted proved that they were the best Santas in the world. Although I would go on in the field of physics, the tales of fantasy and imagination that were in those comic books helped to make me a more complete scientist, unafraid to use my creative as well as my cognitive abilities.

"Is it possible, just possible, that fate can move its huge hand occasionally in even seemingly insignificant ways?" Dr. Ruehl asked rhetorically, before launching into the story of his Santa Miracle.

While shopping with my mother, Florence, right after Thanksgiving at Buffum's Department Store Glendale, California, she admired an eye-catching beige Stetson cowboy hat adorned with a tuft of raccoon fur on one side and a trio of raccoon tails dangling from it on the other side.

I sensed immediately that she had fallen in love with that hat, although she did not try it on. She probably hoped that I would surprise her with it as a

Christmas gift. A collector of hats, each with a nickname, this would have been the ideal present for her.

I returned to the store a few days later, fully intending to purchase the hat. To my great disappointment, someone else had grabbed it. I was kicking myself for procrastinating, especially when the clerk told me they had no more in stock and could not re-order one this close to the holidays.

Embarking on a quest for the hat, I went from one store to another, from small shops to chain department stores, all to no avail. No one had any hat even remotely resembling it. I was berating myself for not going back that first day and buying it.

A few days before Christmas, as I was riding with my dad, Franklin, who had also kept an eye out futilely for that cherished hat, we hit some traffic. Trying to avoid the congestion, he decided to take a right turn that he normally would not have. On our route, we passed by a small boutique I had not seen previously. "Stop!" I cried at my father. While he waited in the car, I dashed inside for one last chance to find that hat.

After a quick examination of their offerings, I didn't find it, and I turned to leave. I was almost to the door when I caught sight of the very gem for which I had been prospecting on the bottom shelf of a glass case! Of course, I immediately purchased it.

As an added surprise, instead of putting it under the Christmas tree, we sneaked it in her closet.

It was not until later on Christmas morning, after opening her other gifts, that she discovered the hat awaiting her, a surprise find that genuinely delighted her. She christened the hat "My Three Raccoons" and has worn it many times with great pleasure, invariably receiving compliments about it.

Amazingly, I talked her into letting me wear the hat for a TV pilot I produced entitled, *The Amazing World of Western Fact and Fiction*. And recently, I have also worn it on a few editions of my webisode, *The Amazing World of Bizarre News*, on Videojug.com. Indeed, a female producer there was pleased with the hat the first time that she saw it and encouraged me to wear it more often!

It is probably presumptuous of me to suggest that fate intervened so that I would find the hat, but my mother and I like to think so, and we regard this a minor Santa Miracle!

Reverend Ann Palmer has affirmed that she has received at least two Santa Miracles—and probably a great many more.

Ann's childhood memories began when our nation was coming out of the Great Depression. "Our family would probably be considered very poor by today's standards," she said, "but we didn't know the difference because nearly every family we knew was facing the same kind of financial problems."

She recalled that her sister and brother were near the same age, and seemed to form a kind of "team" against her, the baby of the family. She jokes that she could have confused her real name with "Tag Along" as that was her older siblings' constant complaint to their father: "Does she have to tag along?"

Her family lived in the Panhandle of Texas, and Ann thinks that from the time she was born they had never visited her parents' relatives who lived in far East Texas. When Ann was five, though, the family planned to visit their relatives for Christmas. Her parents had bought a new car for the trip. "It could have been a used car," Ann considered. "It was a black and shiny Chevrolet, because black seemed to be the only color cars came in in those days."

At age five, Ann recalled that she probably believed in Santa Claus more than Jesus or God. "I was very upset to be driving across Texas on Christmas Eve," Ann said. "How would Santa Claus ever be able to find us while we were on the road?

"Are we there yet?" is certainly a question that children wear out with repetition on a long automobile drive, and Ann remembers asking it many times.

"We must have driven all night and stopped at a restaurant for breakfast," Ann said. "I roused from my sleep in the backseat along with my brother and sister. I was not a happy traveler, sleeping cramped up in the backseat next to my older siblings, and grumbling about how we should be home for Christmas and how Santa would never find them in the middle of Nowhere, Texas."

When the family returned to the car after break-fast, Ann had the surprise of her young life.

"Somehow, Santa had found our car while we had breakfast because as we returned, there in the back seat was a brush and mirror set on the left side of the back seat for my sister, a truck for my brother on the right side and there in the middle was a beautiful doll for me. Maybe there were other trinkets but I don't remember them. The thing I do remember is thinking, 'How could Santa possibly find us while we were traveling in a car across Texas?' To my five-year-old mind, that was the first miracle I had ever experienced."

Since the miraculous visit of Santa when she was five, Ann has experienced many miracles in her life. When she was thirteen she began modeling for major department stores in Dallas. After a few more years of experience, she became a runway model at fashion shows. And then one miracle after another occurred in her life. Ann went to Hollywood and was placed under contract by 20th Century Fox. Within a few months she was in Italy, appearing in the film *Cleopatra* and socializing with the likes of Elizabeth Taylor, Richard Burton, Rex Harrison, and Roddy McDowell. When she returned to the States, she had small parts in such films as *Love with the Proper Stranger* with Steve McQueen and Natalie Wood, *Bonnie and*

Clyde with Warren Beatty and Faye Dunaway, and many others.

Another Santa Miracle occurred for Anne when she was working as a commentator for Cadillac at the new car Motor Shows.

"I had flown in from California to work an auto show in Dallas just before Christmas," Ann recalled. "This job would give me the opportunity to visit my parents for Christmas Eve in their home 30 miles east of Dallas."

At the show, Ann was growing tired of working. "I had trumpeted the wonders of Cadillac automobiles for about six hours," she said. "I got off work at 11:00 P.M. and had to change out of my evening dress before I began the drive to my parents' home. About half way between Dallas and my parents' house, I got a flat tire. I was so tired from stepping in and out of cars all day, but I had to get my strength together and say 'I can do this!'"

Ann got the spare tire out of the trunk and rolled it over to the flat. "I got the car jacked up but when I tried to turn the wrench on the lug nuts, I found I couldn't get the wheel off."

Ann struggled. It could be dangerous flagging down a passerby, especially after midnight on a Saturday night, but she felt she had no choice. She happened to have a pair of red pajamas in her luggage, and she removed them from the suitcase and started waving them—but no one stopped.

"Off in the distance I could see a truck driving toward the highway," Ann said. "I just *knew* it was coming to help me. Sure enough, the truck pulled over and the driver got out of the clean, white medium-sized truck. He was very neatly dressed in a clean uniform. He turned on a large flashlight and showed me that on that particular model, there was a reversed bolt that was sort of inside a hole, which I could not see without a flashlight."

In moments, the courteous truck driver had changed the tire.

"He wouldn't accept money, and he told me not to worry as he would follow me all the way to my parents' house," Anne recalls. She was stunned, because her parents' home was at least 20 miles farther.

On the way to her final destination, Ann resolved to write to the company that employed the driver and tell them what a helpful and courteous driver they employed. She kept looking in the rearview mirror, trying to make out the license number, but she could never quite see it. She decided that she would wait until she turned to her parents' home, and then she would get the name of the company off the side of the truck as he passed her.

"I turned to go to my parents' house, and I stopped to see him pass so I could get the name of the company—but the truck was no longer there," Ann said. "I had seen the headlights and the cab with the smiling driver following me all the way to my parents' home, but now it wasn't there. It had vanished."

Ann realized at that moment that she had been the recipient of a Santa Miracle. "Why was such a neatly dressed truck driver in a pristine white truck going somewhere at midnight on a Saturday night? And why would even the most courteous and thoughtful of truck drivers volunteer to follow me all the way to my parents' home, at least twenty miles out of his way? And, of course, how could such a large truck completely disappear when it was only a couple of car lengths behind me?"

Anne concluded her story, "I know that it was an angel that manifested for my help."

Our friends and fellow authors Jeff Belanger and Megan Peckman Belanger have been collecting stories of children's encounters with Santa Claus. When they learned of *Santa Miracles* they generously sent us the following stories for use in our book.

Betty Jane Medved of Pittsburgh, Pennsylvania, recalled that her first meeting with Santa was in the basement of their church when she was in second or third grade.

"We were in a Sunday school program, singing those little Sunday school songs," Betty Jane recalled. "Nobody ever expected Santa Claus. Even when I look back I'm surprised, because Santa Claus is almost verboten in our church. They don't even talk about him.

"There was a small stage in the basement, and our parents were there. We were all sitting in our seats when the Sunday school director came up and announced, "I have one more surprise for everybody." And here Santa Claus came bounding out onto the stage, waving and ho-ho-ho-ing and everything.

"We just all went crazy, because we never expected him. All of us kids got in a long line, waiting to get up on the stage and talk to him. We were laughing and giggling, jumping up and down, and squealing. It was so much wilder than the excitement that you would have at a department store, because it was such a surprise—and in church, it felt kind of forbidden.

"It was Santa, and he was on the stage at our Sunday School program! We just couldn't believe it. We kept saying to each other, 'It's him! It's him! It's him!'

"And by the time we got up on stage, it had changed to 'It's you! It's you!' Then Santa handed out little presents to everybody.

"I remember looking around for my mother, looking for direction on how I should behave during all this; but she was just laughing and having a good time."

When Elizabeth Judd, from San Francisco, California, was ten, and her brother Shawn was four, he still believed in Santa.

"I hadn't believed for years since I'd seen my dad putting gifts under the tree," Elizabeth said. "On Christmas morning, Shawn woke me up around five to go open presents. My parents, who were still half-asleep, made us lie in bed with them for a while, telling my brother that Santa may not have come yet, so he needed to wait.

"After lying there for a little bit, we all heard a thump on the roof. My brother got *so excited* that Santa was here.

"My parents and I went along with his excitement to add to Shawn's thrill about hearing Santa. Then we heard another thump—and suddenly, a bright red light filled the room as it passed by the window.

"Needless to say, we were shocked. We never figured out what it was, but to this day, my brother still believes it was Santa."

Dave Gotcher from Dallas, Texas, played Santa Claus at Universal Studios Hollywood for five years.

"My favorite memory as a Santa," Dave fondly remembers, "was when I went out with a group of volunteer performers to a place that was basically an adult day care center for senior citizens. That's where I met Frank.

"Frank had a stroke and couldn't speak anymore. An aide wheeled him up to me and said, 'Frank, tell Santa what you want.'

"I watched as this man struggled to try to speak and saw the tears build in his eyes when he couldn't.

"I heard myself say, 'It's all right, Frank. Santa never forgets a friend, and we go way back. I know what you want and I'll do my best. Bless you Frank.'

"I'd *never* said 'bless you' to anyone before. Frank then grabbed me in a hug so tight I thought my ribs would break. We were both crying openly.

"As we were leaving, the nurse said Frank had been unresponsive for a week before that visit.

"I went back the next year, and all they knew was that Frank was no longer there. I sure hope he got that wish."

Norma Joiner, one of our favorite e-mail buddies, recalled growing up in Hawaii, on the island of Kauai, she and her two sisters had great childhood experiences.

"We spent many weekends with family camping on the beach, fishing, swimming in the ocean or a stream, hiking, picking fruits in the mountains, and exploring. There was adventure all the time."

Norma's memories of Santa and Christmas are mingled with recollections of the days in the 1940s and '50s when times were tough and her father worked as a stevedore on the docks.

"My mother was a stay at home Mom, and I remember how washing the laundry meant boiling the water in a large drum, stirring it with a wooden stick, and then rinsing it in another drum filled with cold water. She would wring out the clothes by hand and then hang each item on clotheslines nailed to the side of the house and stretched across the yard to a tree at the side of the garage. Poles were used to lift the lines and raise them to a safe height from the ground. We learned, early on, that laundry days were not the time to play chase in the back yard.

"My father worked long hours and there came a time when he got involved in organizing a union on the docks for better wages and benefits for the minority workers. In representing the workers, he also got involved in special occasions where there were parties.

"One of the memories my sisters and I cherish was helping at Christmas when our living room was crowded with boxes of apples, oranges, nuts, and candies. My two sisters and I would fill brown bags with goodies and make sure everything was counted twice. It was a very exciting time for us as we got to be helpers for the big Christmas party for the families of the stevedores. Our living room smelled wonderful and the feeling of Christmas was alive!

"The night of the party, the stevedores and their families would gather at a large warehouse and there were decorations, a huge tree with lots of presents, and

Santa was there. There was laughter, music, singing, and food.

"Helping my father getting those bags ready so he could play Santa to his men was always the highlight of Christmas at our house. To this day, my sisters and I still remember the smiles on the faces of the children as they got their bags of goodies and a present from Santa.

"We are grateful for a mother and father who taught us at a young age to share with others—and that is a precious gift that no one can ever take away. That was our Santa Miracle."

Well-known as an author of inspirational works, Beverly Hale Watson of Grapevine, Texas, also devotes her time to many charitable groups and organizations, including sending regular packages of gifts and personal items to our men and women serving in Iraq and Afghanistan. Beverly is a firm believer in miracles of all kinds, including Christmas miracles, angel miracles, and Santa Miracles. For this book, she has contributed the timetable during which an extraordinary miracle occurred—and Beverly herself was a participant:

December 22

Anna Thompson was nestled under a heavy down-filled comforter listening to crackling wood and watching embers burn in the fireplace. Cool air flowed through cracks in the barren wood floor as wind whistled through the uncovered window frames. Scattered thoughts filled her mind while she lay in bed. Tomorrow her class was taking a field trip from their school in Virginia to Mallard Creek Mall in Charlotte, North Carolina. She was filled with anticipation, but had other issues on her mind.

Her mother had been hospitalized four times since March with back problems. Her father, Arlis, was a coal miner, who had been laid-off from work in June. Soon their debts exceeded their income and their savings, and put them in bankruptcy. In October, they were evicted from their home. Out of desperation her father had roamed the back roads searching for an abandoned house where they could live. This house was hidden in a holler. The living room, kitchen, and three bedrooms were empty, but each had a beautiful fireplace with logs neatly stacked on the right side. In the backyard he found a well with running water. It wasn't a palace, but certainly better than living out of their van. His family would have a home.

December 23

Anna awoke to the loud buzzing of her alarm clock. The fire had died during the night causing the air to become quite brisk. Getting her muscular arms into position, she quickly lifted her body into the wheelchair sitting next to her bed. Both legs had been amputated above her knees due to an automobile accident.

"It was a drag being confined to this contraption," Anna recalls. But, she had no choice. Although her father wanted to get her artificial legs, he could not afford them. She knew it pained him to see her in the wheelchair. He often prayed that things could be different. For Anna, it was an inconvenience; she hated that people considered her handicapped, but made the best of her situation.

Anna rushed through her normal morning routine, not wanting to miss the school bus.

The bus driver tooted his horn as he drove up the lane leading to her house. She emptied her piggy bank, grabbed her coat and headed for the door. Two hefty boys loaded her onto the bus and strapped her in place; they were happy she only weighed 90 pounds. The bus started on the three-hour journey to Charlotte.

As the students approached Mallard Creek Mall there were traffic jams, impatient people seeking parking spaces, and last minute shoppers scurrying to get inside. "My holler in Virginia is nothing like this!" Anna exclaimed.

Judy Brickle arrived at the mall an hour ahead of schedule. Her youthful appearance, warm smile, and abundance of energy belied her fifty years of age.

She was headed for the large spruce tree decorated with colorful paper angels furnished by The Salvation Army. Each one contained the name and age of a boy or girl, plus their Christmas wish list. Shoppers would stop by, select an angel, purchase the items requested, and return them to the Angel Tree for delivery. It was Judy's job to answer questions, give out angel names, and keep track of the gifts purchased. Every Christmas, she bought gifts for other kids, as she had none of her own. She felt it was always more blessed to give than receive.

Next to the Angel Tree were 500 dolls on display. Each one wore a handmade outfit sewn to perfection. These dolls would be given to some "special angels" whose names were on the tree.

Anna couldn't believe her eyes as she worked her way through the department store aisles in awe of all the Christmas decorations. Her friends couldn't wait to shop. Anna wanted to take her time, so she decided to go it alone.

Quickly she spotted the Angel Tree and the 500 dolls on display next to it. She maneuvered her wheel chair through the crowds and parked herself in front of the display.

Judy noticed Anna and her curly blond hair, small face, and sparkling blue eyes. When she smiled, her deep dimples became even more pronounced. Judy wondered what could have caused one so young to be left without legs.

"The dolls you are looking at are to be given to the girls whose names are on the Angel Tree." Judy commented as she approached Anna. "Which one do you like?" Judy asked, not knowing what else to say.

"I really love the bride doll on the end of the top shelf," Anna answered. "It is beautiful! Her white lace top with all those pearls just glisten under the lights. Her long satin skirt and fluffy petticoats are gorgeous. She even has a crown holding her veil, all trimmed with lace and tiny pearls. You know, I have always wanted a doll like that, but my parents could never afford to buy me one. She looks like something out of a dream!"

As other people approached Judy to ask questions about the Angel Tree, she found herself leaving Anna alone to look at the dolls. Anna would leave the exhibit and then return. Her focus was always on the bride doll she so admired.

As Judy observed this child, she knew in her heart that there had to be some way she could arrange for Anna to receive this doll. Without missing a beat, she reached into her sweater pocket to retrieve a pencil and pad of paper to write down Anna's name and address. She planned to add an angel to the Angel Tree with her name on it.

However, when Judy reached into her pocket it was empty. She forgot that she had left the items on a table on the other side of the tree. Quickly, she headed over to the table to reclaim her pencil and paper.

At that moment, another woman approached Judy requesting information about the Angel Tree. When Judy returned to the doll display, Anna was gone. Frustrated with the way this incident unfolded, Judy was bound and determined to locate Anna in the mall. Anxiously, she waited for the relief volunteer to arrive.

Not wanting to waste any time, Judy removed the bride doll from the display and put it in a box with a blank angel tag on it. Then she contacted me and requested a list of all the schools that had scheduled visits to the mall on that day.

While I was busy securing the requested list of schools, Judy and the relief volunteer continued their search for Anna. They asked other teenagers if they knew her, hoping to obtain her full name, but to no avail, so Judy returned to the Salvation Army's Office.

I arranged for her and two other women to start calling the various schools listed. We were sure it wouldn't be difficult to find Anna because of the fact that she was in a wheelchair.

First they called all the local schools—no matches. Next long distance phone calls were made to schools in surrounding states.

Twenty-three schools down the list and "Bingo"— they had a match! The student was from Tazewell County, Virginia. Judy couldn't believe they had found her.

It was two o'clock, and there was still much to do. Judy quickly relayed what had taken place earlier in the day to the school principal, Mr. Martin. If he would provide her with an address, the bride doll would be mailed tonight for delivery on Christmas Eve. She sincerely needed his assistance in this matter.

"Mrs. Brickle," Mr. Martin said, "I truly want to help you, but there are a few other concerns that we must address. First of all, the Thompson family lives in a holler. They have no street address. The only way the doll would get to her would be if it was sent to me or to my secretary's home. I would be delighted to drop off the doll, but I'm leaving town in the morning. That means it will be up to my secretary to handle this. Secondly, there are three other girls in the family. If you send something for Anna, you really need to include something for the other children so there are no hurt feelings."

"I will be glad to take care of them, too," Judy replied. "Just give me their names and ages. Can you check with your secretary to see if she can deliver the packages?"

The principal put Judy on hold while he telephoned his secretary, Mrs. Wiley. He asked her if it would be possible for her to run by the Thompsons' home that next day.

"I really don't have the time!" Mrs. Wiley answered. "We have company coming in from out of town. I still have presents to wrap, food to prepare, and a house to clean. Plus, the Thompson family lives an hour's drive from my house. I would be happy to do it some other day, but not tomorrow," she replied.

After hanging up the telephone, Mrs. Wiley realized that Christmas was no time to be selfish. Feeling guilty about her response, she quickly picked up the telephone and called her boss back. "I'll be glad to deliver the packages to the Thompsons," she told him. "Just send them to my home address."

By that time, it was four o'clock—time for the kids from Virginia to leave for home. Anna and her friends were headed for the school bus when she decided to go by the doll display for one more glimpse of her dream doll.

As she approached the area, a look of bewilderment came over her face. The doll was gone!

Scanning the display she realized it was the only one not there. "Where could it be?" she wondered.

Anna looked at her watch. She had ten minutes to catch the bus. "Darn, I wish I had returned to the Angel Tree sooner. It would have been wonderful if my three sisters' names could have been added," she thought to herself. Quickly turning her wheelchair around, she zoomed for the exit doors.

As Anna made her journey home, Judy got the names, ages, and "wish lists" of Anna's siblings. Filled with enthusiasm, Judy headed for the nearest department store at the mall. She had ninety minutes to gather up an assortment of clothing and toys and bring them to the gift-wrapping department. While the items were being wrapped, she went to the Angel Tree to pick up four dolls. By the time she returned, the clerk was ready to wrap them.

"These gifts need to be boxed up and shipped overnight delivery," Judy explained to the clerk.

"Sorry ma'am, the mail truck left here fifteen minutes ago," the clerk told her. "I can box the stuff up, but they won't go out until tomorrow."

Judy knew that time was of the essence. "Will you please send the boxes downstairs to Parcel Pick-Up?" she asked the clerk. "I'll take them to the post office myself. Hopefully, I won't be too late to have them put on a truck bound for Virginia."

Her adrenaline was pumping as Judy weaved through hundreds of people moving like a herd of cattle down the escalator. Judy exited the mall and found her car. Everywhere she turned, there was traffic. Cars were moving so slowly. They reminded her of swamp turtles taking a stroll on an extremely hot day.

Thanks to a polite driver who let her cut in line, she inched her way over to Parcel Pick-Up. As Judy approached, a man rushed through the doors before she had a chance to get out of her car.

"Open your trunk, ma'am, and I'll put your boxes inside for you," he remarked. Wasting no time, Judy happily complied.

As she drove the ten blocks to the post office, she prayed that there would be a parking spot near the front door and that the lines would be short inside. She had to get these packages mailed out that night! Judy spotted an open space and wheeled into the slot.

Inside there were people standing in two long lines. Not wanting to waste any time, she got the attention of a supervisor who was willing to assist her. "I need these shipped overnight delivery," Judy explained, sliding the boxes onto the counter.

The packages were heavier than she anticipated, and she was thankful when she could set them down. Other customers voiced their annoyance that she was getting preferential treatment after they had been waiting patiently in line. Judy smiled meekly and continued with her transaction.

"That will be $20.25," said the mail clerk.

Judy opened her purse, pulling out her wallet. All she had was $15.25. "Sir, I am short $5. It is imperative that these packages are shipped out tonight," she said in a desperate voice.

"I 'm sorry lady, I can't ship them until you pay for the postage," he stated firmly, knowing he had to abide by the rules.

Judy's mouth went into high gear. She explained what had happened earlier and why it was necessary that the boxes got out that night.

The mail clerk sympathized with her, but legally he couldn't mail them "overnight delivery" without her paying for them. He would hold the boxes until she came up with the additional $5.

Knowing that he was not going to budge, she headed for her car to see if there was any money in her coat pocket.

Before she left the post office, a stranger approached her. "I couldn't help overhearing what happened to you at the counter," he said. "Here's $5. Don't worry about paying me back, just have a Merry Christmas."

Dumbfounded, Judy thanked the man and ran back to the counter, waving the $5 bill in her hand, yelling to the mailman who had waited on her. He quickly took her money, grabbed her boxes, and headed for the trucks loading up at the back dock. The Virginia-bound truck hadn't left yet.

December 24

Mrs. Wiley's house was filled with friends and relatives. It was all she could do to keep her wits about her. Between preparing food, settling disputes amongst the children, and trying to tend to everyone's needs, her patience was running thin.

Just then the doorbell rang. Her husband opened the door. "Special Delivery," the mailman shouted as he climbed back into his truck. "Have a Merry Christmas."

Mr. Wiley slid the boxes inside the house.

Mrs. Wiley called everyone together and explained what had to be done. Did anyone want to ride out to the Thompsons' place with her?

The response was overwhelming. All ten guests wanted to go and to share in the surprise. After all, the real meaning of Christmas was to bring love, joy, and happiness to others.

Anna and her family were sitting around the fireplace in the living room singing Christmas carols. They didn't have any electricity, so candles and lanterns provided their light. Paper ornaments and popcorn threaded on string decorated their Christmas tree, which Arlis had brought in from the woods. He felt bad that he could not provide better for his family during this time of year. However, considering all that had happened to them, this was a very blessed Christmas. He was thankful for a roof over their heads. Besides they had the necessities and plenty of love.

Hearing a knock on the door, one of Anna's sister rushed to open it. A dozen people were standing on the porch. Some were carrying baskets filled with fruit and food. Others had beautifully wrapped packages tucked under their arms.

"Mrs. Wiley what are you doing here?" she asked totally surprised.

"We just stopped by to wish you a Merry Christmas and deliver some presents for you and your family," she replied.

Tears filled Arlis's eyes as his children jumped up and down, squealing with joy.

"We can't stay and celebrate with you, but do hope you have a wonderful evening." Mrs. Wiley said as she passed along the gifts to the family members.

Excitement filled the air as the girls opened their presents. Anna took her time savoring the moment. She opened her smaller packages first, leaving the largest box to the last.

As she removed the paper from it, tears streamed down her face. It was the beautiful bride doll she had seen at the mall! An angel tag was attached to her dress with this message: *"Please report to Dr. Brickle's office on January 2 at 10:00 A.M. to be fitted for artificial legs. The prostheses and medical services will be provided at no charge. Merry Christmas!"*

As Arlis sat in his chair observing his family, he knew that his prayers had been answered. His family was safe and warm; his children had a real Christmas; and Anna would no longer be in a wheelchair. Indeed, he was a blessed man for he had witnessed the miracle of Christmas.

S ome years ago when we were presenting a seminar in the Los Angeles area in early December, we began to feel in a rather festive mood toward the close of our final session. It was our last seminar of the year, and it was growing close to Christmas. While our topics of the past three days had covered a wide variety of metaphysical subjects, we decided to delve into an area of mysticism that nearly everyone has experienced—a belief in Santa Claus.

"When you were a child," we asked the group collectively, "what one thing made you believe in Santa Claus?" Our question created small explosions of laughter from many of our seminar participants. It wasn't long, though, before many individuals got into the spirit of our question.

While we heard a number of great answers, a few favorites stand out in our memories. Matt told us of the following experience that convinced him of Santa's existence.

"I was only three or so. I saw my older brother and sister writing in their note pads for school, and when I asked them what they were doing, they said that they were writing their letters to Santa Claus. They explained that this was how Santa found out what kids wanted for Christmas. So, naturally, I took a crayon and began to scribble my list on a sheet of paper.

"I remember being very upset when neither my brother nor my sister would take my letter with theirs to school the next day. My sister said not to worry. One of Santa's elves would find my letter and bring it to Santa at the North Pole.

"After they left for school and Mom had me bundled up to go outside and play in the snow banks next to the house in Montana, I toddled to our grove and put my letter to Santa in a hollow in one of the trees.

"When Christmas morning came, I got everything that I had asked for," Matt concluded his story. "That convinced me that Santa could work miracles. One of his elves retrieved my letter and brought it to Santa. That was totally magical and completely convincing in my mind. Of course at that age, it didn't occur to me that my 'letter' was just scribbles and that I might have mentioned what I wanted for Christmas within earshot of Mom or Dad once or twice."

Alyssa is a California girl, and when she was around four, her older sister told her one day that Santa could find out what she wanted for Christmas if she talked into a seashell and threw it as far as she could into the ocean.

Alyssa's parents had taken her to see a department store Santa and young Alyssa had become frightened and started screaming at his first "ho-ho." She thought that she had completely blown it with the Big Man, and she moped around the house in total despair. That was when her sister took her out on the beach one chilly Saturday afternoon and told her about an alternate method of giving Santa your "want list."

"After I thought I had found just the right sea shell," Alyssa remembers, "I shouted all the things that I wanted from Santa into the sea shell just as quickly as I could. I threw it as far as I could into the oncoming tide. My sister cried, 'Good job!'"

Her sister must have been right, as Alyssa got nearly everything that she had asked for from Santa.

"I could only think that Santa was truly a most wonderful miracle worker," Alyssa said. "I mean, even the fish and other creatures of the sea would deliver a kid's Christmas list to him at the North Pole. That was some kind of wonderful."

Ella also had a somewhat unorthodox method of getting her wish list to Santa.

"I grew up on a small ranch in Wyoming," she said. "I watched my older brother Ethan writing his list to Santa just before he left the house and ran for the school bus. Since I was only three at the time, I wasn't quite certain that I understood how the process worked."

Ella's mother explained that Ethan's third grade teacher had asked each of the students to write a letter to Santa Claus. When they brought them to class that morning, the teacher would put them in a special box for direct delivery to Santa.

Ella didn't understand letter writing, but she certainly knew who Santa Claus was.

"Sometime that afternoon," Ella recalls, "I opened the drawer in Mom's dresser where I knew she kept the special stationery that she used when she wrote letters to Grandma in Kansas. Of course, at the time, I just knew that Grandma lived far away, but I knew that it took this special paper to get to her. Such special paper would surely get to Santa."

Ella knew that her mother wouldn't mind if she borrowed a sheet, so she carefully removed a piece of the stationery from the blue cardboard box with the blue ribbon that kept the papers from falling out.

"I told Santa that I wanted a Barbie doll and a toy stove and a bunch of other things that I had seen advertised on television. I ended by telling Santa how much I loved him and Mrs. Santa Claus and all the elves that made the toys."

When Ethan returned from school late that afternoon, Ella showed him her list and asked him to put in the special box to Santa that they had at school.

Ethan laughed and said that Ella's letter was just a bunch of scribbles and squiggles. "Santa can't read that, you little nut," he told her. "And that box for letters to Santa at school is just for us third graders."

When Ella started to cry and sob and wonder how she would let Santa know what she wanted for Christmas, Ethan relented.

"My big brother was always good to me," Ella said, "and when he saw how upset I was, he told me that there was another way to get my wish list to Santa."

Ethan reminded her that the little manger scene that they had on the fireplace mantel had a lot of animals, like sheep, donkeys, and camels along with the wise men, the shepherds, Joseph, Mary, and the baby Jesus.

"You just pick out an animal that you think knows how to pass the word to Santa, and the job gets done," Ethan informed his little sister. "Remember the little song that you sing in Sunday school, 'Away in a Manger'? Remember what it says about the cattle waking Baby Jesus? We got a lot of cattle on this ranch."

Ethan walked Ella down to the pen where some of the calves that were being weaned from the milking cows were kept. He told her to watch them carefully, pick the one that looked the most trustworthy, and whisper her list in its ear.

"It was pretty easy to whisper in the calves' ears," Ella explained, "because it was feeding time and one of Ethan's chores was to see that the calves got fed. Five or six of them were sticking their heads out between the boards of the pen."

It didn't take Ella long to pick the one that she felt was most capable of beginning the long line of communication to Santa Claus. "We had Hereford cattle on the range," she explained, "and some Guernsey cattle for milking. I picked the calf with brown patches over his eyes that made him look very wise."

And the animal telephone system obviously worked, Ella laughed. She got everything she wanted for Christmas that year.

Ella recalls fondly, "I whispered my Santa list into a calf's ear every year until I was in second grade,"

Hunter was quite a bit older than some of our seminar participants and he could remember a radio program back in the late 1930s or early 1940s that had a bear with a high tenor singing voice who could place direct messages to Santa by having the North Wind carry them to him in the North Pole.

"I think this singing bear was called 'the Cinnamon Bear,' but I could be misremembering," Hunter said. "Anyway, I was very much taken with the program. It came on right after school, and I couldn't get into any snowball fights or build any snowmen or construct any snow forts if I wanted to get home in time to hear the latest updates on Santa's workshop progress from the Cinnamon Bear."

Hunter was in second grade, and had no trouble writing his letter to Santa. "Maybe all the words weren't spelled correctly," he conceded, "but I figured Santa or one of his elves could make out all of my Christmas wishes."

Completely convinced by the Cinnamon Bear's testimonial for the efficiency of the North Wind to deliver children's Christmas lists to Santa, Hunter found the highest spot around him on a windy day and let his letter fly to the North Pole.

She had sat up late one Christmas Eve, hoping to see Santa.

Her parents warned her that Santa wouldn't come as long as she sat cuddled up in her blankie on the sofa.

"I am the first to concede that I was a rather willful child when I was four," Hailey said, "but I was determined to sit up all night so that I might see Santa at work. I was also going to check off the items on my list to see if he had brought everything that I wanted."

Hailey was sound asleep by ten o'clock or so, but when she awakened during the night, she saw a most astonishing sight.

"There, moving around the Christmas tree, were two balls of light, one red, one green," she recalled.

"They bobbed up and down around the tree, and I knew that I was watching Santa and one of his elves bringing the presents."

There was a part of Hailey that wanted to jump off the sofa and run to hug Santa and tell him how much she loved him. "But I knew better than to make a single peep," Hailey said, "or up the chimney they would go, taking my presents along with them. I had been warned about the great, inviolable rule that no child was allowed to see Santa or his elves in the act of putting presents around the Christmas tree or in the Christmas stockings, so I snuggled deep under the cover of my blankie. I think I might even have snored just a little bit to convince Santa and his elf that I was really sleeping."

When Hailey awakened the next morning, she was in her bed.

"I ran downstairs and told Mommy and Daddy that I had really seen Santa and his elf putting the presents under the tree," Hailey said. "Both of them kind of scolded me and said that I was very lucky that Santa didn't know that I was awake. I told them that I made certain that Santa and his elf thought I was asleep by making little snoring sounds.

Growing up, Andrea's grandfather had her convinced that Santa miracles filled every day in December.

"Grandpa Lars's hobby was magic," Andrea told us. "As a child, he had me completely convinced that the world was filled with wonder and excitement at every turn. During the Christmas season, he was at his height of glory. Every night after he returned from his job as an accountant, he would transform himself into The Wonderful Wizard of Oz or of Copenhagen or of somewhere. He had been an actor who had appeared in amateur stage productions in Denmark, so he was also very skilled in the art of theatrical makeup."

Andrea explained that when she was four, she and her mother lived with Grandma and Grandpa

Kristofferson while her father was serving in Korea in 1950. She missed her father very much, and the entire family watched the war news every night. Andrea could tell that her mother was very worried about the situation, and each night at bedtime, they would pray for her father's safe return.

"In this time of great emotional stress for my mother and me, Grandpa Lars literally created an alternate reality for me," Andrea remembers. "I will always, always, bless him for that."

Every Christmas Eve, Grandpa would manage somehow to slip away on an "errand" and change into his Santa Claus suit. Soon, seemingly from out of nowhere, Santa would suddenly appear beside the Christmas tree and begin to pass out presents.

"He was such a master of makeup that I never once even guessed that Santa Claus was really Grandpa," Andrea laughs. "Remember, I was only four years old. Then, a little while later, after Santa had taken off again in his sleigh, Grandpa would come back with a sack of groceries or something in his hands to explain his absence from the scene when Santa was there. Grandpa would stomp one of his feet and moan, 'Oh, no! Did I miss him again?'"

In 1952, God blessed the Kristofferson family with the safe return of Andrea's father from the Korean conflict. In a few more months, Dad had returned to the

Minnesota city in which they lived, and he got an apartment for them not far from Andrea's grandparents.

"When I was older, I understood that the proximity to my grandparents' home was a matter of necessity," Andrea told us. "Both Dad and Mom had to get jobs to get the family on its feet, and it was convenient for me to be able to stop at Grandma's after school to stay until Mom or Dad came home to take me to our apartment."

Andrea reminded us that she was now six, going on seven, and stated that, like most children of that age, she had begun to hear some ugly rumors about Santa Claus at school. After dinner one night at her grandparents, she confronted her grandfather with the gossip going around the playgrounds at recess that there was no Santa Claus.

"Grandpa Lars's eyes widened and he looked at me as if I had just said a naughty word in church," Andrea recalled with an infectious laugh. "He assured me that there most certainly was a Santa Claus and all those kids who were spreading such awful stories were very sadly mistaken."

Andrea said that her beloved grandfather's reassurances steeled her against the most advanced logic that any of her classmates could put forward about Santa Claus not being real.

On Christmas Eve, Andrea and her parents joined Grandma and Grandpa Kristofferson in their home to decorate the tree. As usual, Grandpa Lars excused himself, saying that he had forgotten to pick up a couple of items at the market.

Only this time, after her grandfather had been absent for a few minutes, Andrea heard a strange scuffling sound in a back room. As she listened more closely, she thought her heard Grandpa Lars groaning.

"My curiosity had reached the bubbling over point," Andrea said, "so I followed the peculiar grunts and groans to a back room that Grandma and Grandpa very seldom used. I opened the door and was shocked to see Grandpa Lars trying to pull on the bright red trousers of a Santa Claus suit."

For a moment, Andrea said that she was struck speechless. Then with a pitiful cry of shock and despair, she managed to blurt out, "Grandpa Lars! What are you doing? Are you pretending to be Santa? Does this mean . . ."

Grandpa Lars shushed her. "Honey," he said, "it's not what it looks like. I got word that Santa was running late to our house, and he asked me to fill in for him until he got here. And these darn red trousers are just too tight."

Andrea stood there, her head swirling with confusion. "Have you . . . I mean, are you Santa? I mean, have you always pretended to be Santa?"

She had barely uttered those words and asked that damning question when a loud voice boomed behind her: "Of course, not, little girl! I'm Santa Claus!"

Andrea whirled around to behold a very large, very plump man in a bright red Santa Claus suit with a bag over his shoulder coming in through the back door.

"It's a wonder that I didn't faint," Andrea said. "I was seeing the real Santa with his bright red cheeks, his full white beard, his red cap and his red suit! The rest of the night was a blur of excitement."

Andrea has a dim memory of Santa leading her by the hand back to the living room and the Christmas tree. Everyone in the family greeted Santa, and he had a present for everyone. And then he was gone.

"But I had seen the real Santa," Andrea said. "He had taken me by the hand. I had felt him, seen him, heard him. And Santa was *not* Grandpa, that was for certain."

When he was a senior in high school, Jimmy worked in a drugstore as a clerk, errand boy, stock boy, and occasional cashier.

"In other words, I worked wherever Mr. Rodriguez, the manager, needed me on that particular day," Jimmy said. "There were days when I really didn't think he needed me at all. There were three other regular employees. But he was a kind man, and he knew that our family was running on empty financially. I really needed to bring home any money that I could to help Pop and Mom with the bills that had accumulated after my little brother Brandon got hit by a car when he was walking home from school in

October. Both legs were broken and he had needed back surgery."

On December 22, Mr. Rodriquez asked Jimmy if he would be able to work on Christmas Eve until the early closing hours of 8:00 P.M. "I wasn't scheduled to work that night," Jimmy said, "but one of the employees, Hilda, had four kids and asked if she could leave at noon to begin preparing a big Christmas dinner for her family. I agreed, because I really needed the extra hours."

Jimmy knew that his own family would like to have him home early in the afternoon, but he also was quite aware of their financial bind and that his parents would be grateful for his willingness to earn a few extra dollars.

Jimmy did throw in one condition for his working late. "I asked Mr. Rodriquez if I could have the big, life-sized plastic Santa Claus that stood next to the Christmas cards on Aisle 13. It was Christmas Eve. We wouldn't need Santa to encourage shoppers to buy Christmas presents after that night, and I knew that Brandon would really get a charge out of having Santa come home with me on Christmas Eve."

Mr. Rodriquez smiled and nodded his agreement. "I only wish I had a sleigh and eight tiny reindeer for you to take home to Brandon, as well!"

About half an hour before closing, Jimmy saw three boys that he knew very casually at high school come into the store. Jimmy knew that they were trouble.

"They were thugs, plain and simple," Jimmy said. "Their black leather jackets announced to the outside world that they belonged to the Trompers. "The first time I saw a couple of those creeps, I thought they had misspelled the word 'Troopers' on the back of their jackets," Jimmy said. "Then I found out from my best friend Mason that 'tromp' was just another word for 'stomp.'"

One of the hoodlums recognized Jimmy from high school and called the others attention to the skinny kid behind the cash register.

"Hey, Jimbo," he chuckled as he swaggered up to the cash register, "you got change for a hundred?"

The other two gang members joined in their buddy's little joke by laughing as if he had just uttered the funniest joke ever heard.

Jimmy didn't answer the smart-guy's question, but he kept an eye on the trio as they moved through the store.

Mr. Rodriquez was busy filling prescriptions, and the other two clerks were helping customers with last-minute Christmas shopping.

Deftly, with practiced skill, the three Trompers shoved packages of cigarettes, candy bars, and several bottles of an expensive perfume under their jackets, then, casually, began to head for the front door.

"Hey, you guys, put the stuff you stole back or I'll call the police," Jimmy yelled as they neared the cash register.

The three Trompers looked as surprised as if a dog had suddenly spoken to them.

"Now you wouldn't want to do that, Jimbo," one of the trio warned him. "Really bad things happen to punks who mess with the Trompers."

Jimmy didn't back down. "The forefinger of my left hand is on a red button," he informed them. "If you guys don't take the stuff you stole out of your jackets, I push the button and the cops will be here before you can get away."

"Hey, Jimbo, where's your Christmas spirit?" The comedian among them tried another little joke. "This here stuff we took are your Christmas presents to us."

Jimmy didn't display the slightest sign of emotion when he fibbed and told the thugs that he had already pushed the button that would summon the police. The Trompers dropped their loot on the floor and ran out of the drug store, bombarding Jimmy with a firestorm of curses that could have singed his hair.

Mr. Rodriquez came out from behind the prescription counter and walked up to the cash register. "I didn't see everything that happened, Jimmy," he said, "but judging from all the things that I see on the floor, I think you just stopped a robbery in progress. Good man, Jimmy."

Jimmy admitted that he was more than a little nervous when he left the store later that night after closing. From what he had heard around high school, the Trompers enjoyed demonstrating how the name of their gang originated.

Jimmy shifted the large plastic Santa that Mr. Rodriquez had given him from arm to arm, hoping to remain on the ready if he should get jumped by the hoods between the store and his car in the parking lot.

Jimmy walked to his car without incident. No tires slashed. No paint scratched by keys. And no one was anywhere to be seen in the lot.

Jimmy put the large image of Santa on the passenger seat, then walked around to the driver's side, careful to scan every shadow in the lot as if it were a potential attacker. All clear.

His next worry was that the nearly twenty-year-old Chevy wouldn't start, but the motor jumped right into mechanical action as he turned the key in the ignition.

When he arrived home, he was pleased that his mother had kept a chicken dinner warm for him in the oven—and he was moved almost to tears by the reception that the life-sized Santa received from Brandon.

"Mom and Dad were pleased, too," Jimmy said. "They said that the Santa Claus that I had brought home would always be a part of the family Christmases."

Christmas Day, late in the afternoon, Jimmy got a telephone call from his friend Mason, asking him details about the run-in with the Trompers the night before. Jimmy was stunned that news had traveled so fast among the teenaged community.

Jimmy told Mason all about what had happened the night before.

"So who did you get to be your bodyguard on the drive home?" Mason asked.

When Jimmy told Mason he had no idea what he was talking about, his friend told him that the Trompers had been waiting in their car for Jimmy to leave the drugstore. They had intended to follow him until he got on the old park road, then force him over, and beat the living daylights out of him. But when the Trompers had edged their car up close behind Jimmy's, they saw that he had someone with him, some really big guy, so they pulled back and decided to jump him sometime when he was alone.

"You know those punks always like to outnumber someone at least three to one before they jump him," Mason said. "They decided your buddy looked too big for them to handle. So who the heck was he?"

Jimmy laughed as he told Mason that he was protected by Santa Claus: a big, life-sized, plastic image of good old St. Nick. From the back, in the beam of the Trompers' headlights, the store decoration must have looked like a real person.

Mason enjoyed the joke on the Trompers, but Jimmy was still worried about the threat of the hoods jumping him and beating him up.

"You got two Santa Miracles on Christmas Eve. After they decided to let you go for the time being, those thugs decided to rob a liquor store. The owner had been robbed twice before, so he was ready for trouble. He held them frozen in their tracks with a double-barreled shotgun until the police arrived. Those jerks will get put away for quite a while in some juvenile prison."

Jimmy still worried about the rest of the gang.

"Looks like you got three Santa Miracles," Mason said, "The three tough guys weren't so tough when the police leaned on them a bit. They gave up the address of the Trompers' hangout, and the other two hoods in the gang are also in the slammer."

Jimmy thanked Mason for the terrific news and enjoyed his day off with his family.

Jimmy concluded his story by stating that when he came back to work after Christmas, Mr. Rodriquez gave him a raise because of the way that he had handled a potential robbery.

Beaming from ear to ear, Jimmy said, "I actually received four Santa Miracles that year."

Kenneth's Santa Miracle is one of the strangest ones that we have ever heard.

"In 1955, my cousin Russ and I were really dyed-in-the-wool UFO buffs, though they called them 'flying saucers' in those days," Kenneth began his strange story. "We were both fourteen that summer and we saw every flying saucer movie released and read every flying saucer book we could find. Our parents—our mothers are sisters—thought we had lost our marbles over flying saucers, but Russ and I considered ourselves serious investigators."

It was their Christmas tradition to meet in the very large and beautifully furnished family lodge in northern Wisconsin that had been built by their great-grandfather, who had arrived from Sweden a wealthy man and soon tripled his income in the New World.

"I lived in Milwaukee and Russ lived in a little town near La Crosse," Ken explained, "so family gatherings were a great time for us to get together and spend hours talking about our research. Otherwise, we had to rely on letters, and a once-a-week telephone call, limited to fifteen minutes. Besides the excitement of Christmas, Russ and I were revved up to go out into the woods, because there had been a bunch of flying saucer reports from that area of Wisconsin."

Once all the families had arrived, the two cousins isolated themselves from the rest of the kids in one of the upstairs bedrooms. In retrospect, Ken realizes that he and Russ were extremely rude to their cousins—including Russ' younger brother, Ken's older sister, and three other female cousins—but they had important research to discuss.

"It gets dark early in northern Wisconsin in December," Ken said. "Since we only had about an hour of daylight, Russ and I decided to go out and get the lay of the land so when we went out after dinner, we'd already have our posts picked where we could scan the night sky."

There was a fresh fall of snow, so neither of them feared getting lost in the thick stand of woods. They could just follow their tracks back to the cabin.

Being "city boys," Ken admitted, they had forgotten that deer, raccoons, and bears also made tracks in the snow when they walked around in the woods.

And, then, just as if the environment followed a strict sense of rules, the woods suddenly became very, very dark about a quarter to five.

Just as quickly, a strong wind began to roar through the trees.

"Where did that wind come from?" Russ wondered, adding: "I think we should get back to the lodge."

Ken agreed that was an excellent idea, but it soon came down to a hard reality that neither of them knew where they were.

"We haven't gone that far into the woods," Russ said. "Our tracks should be easy to follow."

Ken agreed.

In spite of their confidence, their flashlights could pick up only a hodge-podge of both four-legged and two-legged footprints.

And then the beam of their flashlights picked up something very intimidating to two young boys lost in the woods. It was beginning to snow.

Russ and Ken were both fourteen, but Ken remembers quite clearly that he felt very much like crying.

"And then we saw it," Ken said. "The very Holy Grail for which we yearned to see for so long: a flying saucer."

Ken pointed to the dark sky and Russ saw it also. A brightly glowing ball of light, perhaps a yard or so in circumference, was bobbing up and down near the top branches of a tall tree.

"I thought they would be larger," Russ whispered.

"They come in all sizes," Ken said, attempting to sound authoritative.

As if it had been eavesdropping on their conversation, the brilliant orb dropped down to skim near the tops of their heads.

Ken and Russ both shouted in terror.

Seemingly satisfied with their response, the flying saucer moved just ahead on them on the trail, then seemed again to be bobbing up and down.

"I think it wants us to follow it," Russ said, a slight waver of fear distorting his voice.

"Maybe it will soon open up and some aliens will come out and grab us."

Ken argued that for aliens to be passengers in that orb, they would only be a few inches tall.

"Maybe it will expand into a huge craft," Russ suggested nervously.

Ken said that he liked Russ' interpretation of the object's bobbing up and down as a gesture to follow it much better than the abduction scenario that he was spinning.

"The light is so bright, we won't stumble in the brush," Ken argued. "What do we have to lose? We're already lost."

The brilliant orb stayed just far enough ahead of the boys to safely lead them out of the woods. By this time, Ken said, they really didn't think it was a flying saucer. They had no idea what it was.

"But within what I would guess to be ten or fifteen minutes, we could see the lights of Great-Grandpa's lodge ahead of us," Ken said.

Simultaneously with the boys' sighting of their family lodge, the glowing object soared high into the night sky, so high, in fact, that Ken and Russ thought that it looked like a star.

"But it wasn't finished with its display of power and majesty," Ken said. "It was like it was showing off for us. It came zooming back down, faster than we could imagine anything flying, and seemed to crash into the lodge."

Ken and Russ screamed in horror. It seemed to them that the mysterious object had led them back to the lodge, only to destroy it. Clearly, from where they stood, the great hall of the lodge was filled with flames.

As the boys got closer to the lodge, running as fast as possible in the ankle-length snow, they saw that they were mistaken. The bright lights inside were streaming from the Christmas tree that the other members of the family had decorated while the boys were out hunting flying saucers in the woods.

When Ken and Russ entered the lodge, they received the anticipated scolding from their mothers for missing the trimming of the Christmas tree. "However," Ken said, "they were relieved and thankful that we hadn't got lost in the woods. They had heard the weather forecast only minutes before and a major storm warning had been issued for that region.

"Russ and I just looked at each other in complete, almost reverent, silence," Ken said. "Whatever that glowing object was, it had saved our lives by leading us back to the lodge before the big snow storm hit. As lost as we were in the woods, we would have been frozen snowmen before any search parties found us. And that would be a terrible way to spend Christmas, frozen like a popsicle."

Ken said that his and Russ' enthusiasm for researching flying saucers was only heightened by the strange experience that they had undergone in the woods that Christmas. But they had many long discussions concerning what they had actually seen that night.

After a great deal of research, they began to consider that they may not have interacted with a spacecraft from an extraterrestrial world, but some mysterious glowing object piloted by elf-like or fairy creatures.

On the other hand, they would laugh, why couldn't it have been Santa Claus and his elves in their own high-tech transport?

Everything seemed just fine to Ronald Griffin when his family moved to an old house in a suburb of Flint, Michigan. Ron's father had been transferred because of his job, and the family moved in time for Ron and his sister Donna to start school at the beginning of the semester.

"Donna was in ninth grade that year and I was in seventh," Ron explains. "We were both really nervous that first day in school. We had lived in Indianapolis before we moved, and we had always lived in the same neighborhood and gone to the same school with class-mates that we had known since we were little kids. It is really difficult to just up and move to a different city, state, and school when you are a kid."

Donna and Ron quickly learned that their fears were unjustified. They both made new friends on the first day, and they received none of the teasing that they worried they might as "new kids." Within the first week of school, each had friends come home with them to watch television and have cookies and milk as an after-school treat.

After dinner, one night when Donna and Ron had gone to their rooms to do homework, Donna knocked on Ron's door and asked if she could come in.

After she settled herself comfortably in his bean-bag chair, she asked what kinds of things he and Logan talked about over cookies and milk.

Ron remembers shrugging and answering "just stuff."

Then Donna came right to the point. "Briana said today that the reason that Daddy got such a good buy on this house was because it is haunted."

Ron laughed. "Haunted?" he echoed. "She must have been kidding you. Just trying to get a rise out of you. Maybe that's the way kids in this town initiate the newbies."

Donna also laughed off the suggestion that there were spooks in their house as "ludicrous." She prided herself on learning a new vocabulary word every day.

The next day in school, Ron told Logan what Briana had said about their home being haunted. Logan snorted derisively and dismissed such a statement as something that a silly junior high school girl would say.

"The house sat empty for quite awhile after old man Fredericson died a couple of years ago," Logan theorized. "That old guy must have been nearly a hundred years old. He was really a nice man. He would stand in his walker on his porch and give out Christmas treats to kids. It would be just like some weirdo girls to come up with a haunted house story and say that the ghost of old man Fredricson was still clumping the house around in his walker."

Ron admitted that even though Briana might well be a "silly junior high school girl," he was a bit on guard as he moved through their house after dark.

"I didn't really believe in ghosts," he said, "but on the other hand, I had read some books about stranger than science stuff, and I had seen some really spooky movies. I watched *The X-Files* and Fox Mulder believed in ghosts, and he was a very cool guy."

But, as Ron began his account, nothing eerie or spooky visited their home until the first week in December.

"I was brushing my teeth before school one day, and Donna came up behind me and slapped me on the back," Ron said. "She was warning me for the last time not to mess with her collection of horse figurines."

Ron protested that he hadn't touched her precious little glass horses, and Donna had screamed in rebuttal that there surely hadn't been an earthquake to move them around on their selves.

Then Ron counterattacked with the accusation that maybe she was putting on some weight and jarring the floorboards of her room so the little horsies bounced all over the shelves.

It was at that point that their mother put her head in the bathroom and told them both to stop fighting and finish getting ready for school.

The next incident occurred two nights later when Donna asked Ron to turn down his radio because she was studying for a history test.

Ron yelled back that he wasn't listening to his radio. He had a test of his own the next day.

In about half an hour, Donna came storming into Ron's room, yelling that she loved Christmas music as much as the next person, but to turn down his radio or she would throw it out the window.

"She kind of turned pale when she was in my room and could see and hear that my radio stood mute at my bedside," Ron said.

"Don't you hear that music," Donna whispered. "Right now. Hear it? 'Jolly Old St. Nicholas' is playing."

Ron felt a genuine shiver go up his back. "When I really stopped to listen, I could hear the music. It was faint and sounded like it was coming from faraway, but I could hear it."

The obvious first place to look was downstairs to check if Mom and Dad were watching a television program that featured music of the holiday season. As it turned out, they were watching a basketball game.

Just at the point where Ron and Donna felt like they were going crazy, the music stopped.

"But the music returned almost every night at about the same time and continued for about an hour," Ron said. "Every night, from about nine until ten, we were serenaded with Christmas music."

After enduring two or three nights of the mystery, they called Mom and Dad upstairs to hear it. Dad never admitted that he could hear it, but Mom said it must be one of the neighbors listening to music before bedtime.

How can we hear music from a neighbor's house?

They must have the window open.

In December?

Maybe it's someone who likes fresh air and likes to sleep in a really cold bedroom.

"We went back and forth like that for several minutes," Ron said, "and then Dad came up with an explanation. He had once upon a time read somewhere that old water pipes and other fixtures could sometimes pick up radio stations. This was an old house with old plumbing. He bet that was the explanation."

Ron and Donna had an hour concert of Christmas music nearly every night. Some nights, he remembered, the music was louder than other nights.

"On the nights when there was no music, Donna and I would be waiting on edge for it to begin," Ron said. "Those nights of silence were actually worse, because we just kept waiting for it to start up again."

After about ten days of intermittent concerts of Christmas music, Donna found the first card.

"Oh, how beautiful, Ron," Donna said one morning. "Did you put this card on my dresser?"

It was a lovely Christmas card with an antique flavor, suggestive of the turn of the century or perhaps the 1920s. Charming it was, but Ron hadn't placed it in his sister's room.

Nor did he place the next six cards in her room, either.

Mom and Dad denied doing so, as well.

Donna and Ron theorized that it must be his friend Logan, who had developed quite an obvious crush on her. He was probably slipping into Donna's room when he came by after school to study with Ron.

"So we checked Donna's room carefully after Logan left one night," Ron said. "There was no card there then or when Donna went to bed—but there was a card awaiting her on her dresser when she awakened."

By this time, Ron admitted, Donna and he were getting pretty freaked out. Their house was haunted. Briana was no silly teenager, after all.

On the other hand, if they had a ghost in the house, it was a nice one. It was a ghost who liked Christmas music and Christmas cards.

One night, just before Christmas vacation, when Ron and Donna sat talking in her room, Ron jokingly said that he hoped the ghost wasn't peeking at him in the shower and that he was kind of jealous because Donna got all the cards.

When he returned to his room, he found two cards at the foot of his bed.

"I barely slept at all that night," Ron said. "I really gave my best Fox Mulder pitch to Mom and Dad that there was a ghost in the house, but they explained everything away –they just thought we and our friends were playing jokes on each other."

The first day of school vacation, Ron and Donna had their mother drop them off at the mall so they could begin their Christmas shopping.

One of the places they enjoyed most at the mall was a shop just off the food court that had been made to look as much as possible like an old-fashioned ice cream and soda parlor. After they had their favorite sundaes in hand, they sat down at a glass-topped table on wire-backed chairs, replicas of popular soda fountain furniture from decades gone by.

An elderly gentleman who sat squeezed in the crowded shop with his shoulders nearly touching Ron's asked if they were "new kids in town"?

"We moved to town that fall, in time for the beginning of the school semester." In the spirit of holiday cheer, he asked the man if he, too, were a "new kid in town"?

The man laughed, introduced himself as William, and said that he was once a new kid in town about seventy years ago. His family had moved to the Michigan city from Indianapolis when he was 10 years old.

With that common ground of origin, the three began to laugh and joke with one another. When William asked where they lived, Donna supplied their address.

"Oh, my goodness," the man laughed. "You live in Father Christmas's old place."

"As we listened, with our mouths hanging open our new friend told us that Mr. Fredricson was called Father Christmas by all his neighbors because of his love of Christmas. Way back in the 1930s, William said, Fredricson had his house covered with lights and his lawn decorated with images of Santa and his sleigh and a small army of elves."

As Ron and Donna sat there spellbound, their elderly friend regaled them with lovely story after story of Mr. Fredricson's love of Christmas and his generosity toward everyone—men, women, and especially children. Dressed in full regalia in a very elaborate Santa Claus suit, Fredericson would drop off boxes of food, toys, and clothing to needy families. In that very same Santa Claus suit, he would stand on his porch on Christmas Eve day and give out candy canes to every kid who came to his door.

Fredricson had no children of his own, but his love for his wife was legendary in the city. The story was that he gave his wife a Christmas card and a small gift on every day of the month from December 1 to the 25.

During the War years of the 1940s, Fredericson had to tone down the lights a bit because of the occasional blackout, but, dressed in his Santa Claus suit, he would drop off boxes of toys on the doorstep of every family whose father was serving in the Armed Forces. In December 1945, the lights shone brightly from the Fredricson house once again. And they continued, until 1991 when Mr. Fredricson died.

Donna asked William if he had ever heard any stories about the house being haunted.

William laughed and said that he wouldn't be at all surprised. Especially around Christmastime.

"When Donna and I got home that evening, we seemed to have some unspoken agreement that passed between us that we should go up to the attic," Ron said. "I suppose Mom and Dad had been up there to inspect the roof before they bought the house, but Donna and I had never investigated the area."

Because there were no lights in the attic, Ron and Donna walked up the steep stairs with flashlights in hand.

"Over in a corner, we found a pile of boxes that didn't belong to our family," Ron said. "In one of them, we found several cartons of old Christmas cards."

"Enough for eternity," Donna whispered over his shoulder.

On Christmas Eve, after the family returned from church services, Ron and Donna went up to their rooms to change out of their dress clothes into sweatshirts and jeans.

"On each of our desks," Ron said, "we found an old-fashioned pressboard figure of Santa, like they used to make during the thirties. The paint on each of them seemed as bright as new. Donna and I had seen them up in the attic when we had found the cards. We didn't need to ask Mom and Dad if they had brought the Santas downstairs. We knew that it was a gift from Father Christmas."

It is often said that no good deed goes unnoticed, but in the case of Ted Horn, waiter, cook, and the owner of Dixie Diner, he had no idea that a simple act of kindness displayed toward a customer in need, would be the inspiration for none other than Santa himself.

Larry Stewart worked as a door-to-door salesman in the small town of Bruce, Mississippi. When the company went out of business, Larry soon found himself out of money. He was so broke that he went for days without having the money to even eat. Cold, desperate, and hungry, Larry wandered into Ted Horn's diner and ordered himself a big breakfast, not disclosing that he didn't have any money to pay for it.

When the time came for the bill to be presented, Larry went to reach for his wallet, then pretended to discover that it was missing. Conducting a search of all possible pockets where his wallet might have been "misplaced," Larry played out his little drama of how embarrassed he was that he should find himself in such an awkward situation.

Ted Horn, chief bottle-washer, cook, waiter, and diner owner, walked over to the stool where Larry was sitting and bent down to pick something up off the floor. Ted straightened back up, with money in hand, looked Larry straight in the eyes, and with no hint that he was on to the missing wallet scheme, he placed a $20 bill on the table in front of him, saying: "Son, you must have dropped this."

That $20 bill was a fortune to Larry as he paid for his breakfast, left a tip, said a silent prayer of thanks. As he walked out of that diner, he pushed his car to a gas station and was able to buy enough gas to get out of town.

While driving, Larry became aware of his thoughts drifting back to the diner, in an attempt to reconstruct his "lucky break." In an aha moment, he realized that nobody else in the diner had dropped that $20 bill. It must have been a deliberate act, out of the kindness and graciousness of the Dixie Diner owner.

Right there and then, Larry Stewart promised himself that if the Lord would ever put him in the position to help others in such a manner, he would do it. And indeed he did. Over the years, Larry Stewart was to settle in the Lee Summit, Missouri area, marry, have a family, and work his way into a major change of fortune. Eventually he would become a *millionaire*.

Years later, Stewart began giving cash to the needy, but remembering the way *his* dignity was spared, he gave birth to the idea of being a *Secret Santa*—disguising himself in the full regalia of Santa Claus and handing out money to people who appeared to be in need, whether he found them in a Laundromat, or on the street, or in a shelter. Feeling the joy, warmth, and glow deep in his heart and soul, Larry knew this would be how he would fulfill his promise. It would be his *mission* to be a Secret Santa.

His wishing to remain anonymous as Secret Santa would affect the lives of thousands upon thousands of people in need, launching what was to become the largest world-wide Secret Santa movement and foundation.

He did not forget the random act of kindness that started it all, as he retraced and tracked down Horn almost thirty years after their first fateful meeting. Stewart found him in Tupelo, Mississipi, and handed eighty-eight-year-old Ted Horn an envelope containing $10,000!

In March 2008, a trained archeologist made a fascinating discovery in the Nine Mile Canyon in central Utah. There, high on the side of a sheer cliff, Pam Miller, Chair of the Nine Mile Canyon Coalition, found a petroglyph, at least 1,000 years old, that clearly appeared to depict Santa, an elf, and nine reindeer.

A petroglyph is a work of art that was chiseled into rock, most often into a dark patina surface by a prehistoric artist. In the case of the ancient Santa Claus and crew in Nine Mile Canyon, the picture had to be chiseled or pecked into rock by some anonymous—and ancient—Native American craftsman.

Did some long-forgotten tribal artist see the original Santa Claus and an elf as they stopped to feed and water the reindeer on their way back to the North Pole? The artist who captured this momentous sighting on rock might have been a member of the tribe of the Shoshone, the Hopi, the Zuni, the Paiute, all of whom, among other early tribes, visited or occupied the area around Nine Mile Canyon.

Interestingly, the Santa petroglyph is located very high on a sheer cliff in a very rugged area of the canyon. Photographer Bill Bryant managed to photograph "Santa" using a super-telephoto lens.

Archaeologist Pam Miller told Cathy Zander of *Newswire* that the aboriginal artist quite likely did not have Santa, an elf, and Santa's particular team of reindeer in mind when he made the petroglyphs. The beauty of such rock art, she emphasized, is that future generations can be inspired by it.

According to Ms. Miller, Santa Claus and his helpers is but one of 10,000 petroglyphs to be found in Nine Mile Canyon. At the time of the announcement of the unique discovery, the Nine Mile Canyon Coalition was doing its best to alert the public that the petroglyphs and pictoglyphs (prehistoric paintings) were in danger of being obliterated or destroyed by heavy industrial traffic, including massive trucks, drill rigs, bulldozers, and trucks spraying dust-suppressant chemicals. The drilling for possible oil deposits in the Nine Mile Canyon area could quite possibly destroy the unique petroglyph of Santa Claus—and all the other priceless works of prehistoric Native American art. Perhaps the public, once alerted to the possible obliteration of these many ancient masterworks, may perform a Santa Miracle and work to preserve this national treasure.

On the other hand, in spite of the learned archaeologists and their many theories, could not this discovery signify more than some intellectual curiosity? May it not beg the question: How long has Santa Claus really been around?

If nothing else, the discovery of this petroglyph gives evidence of the multicultural diversity of Santa Claus and the innate spiritual truth of an unselfish, giving spirit. And interestingly, the estimated age of the Santa petroglyph is very close to time when he began to appear in Europe—and may even predate his earliest manifestation in France.

L ori Jean Flory remembers Christmas best for the
Santa Miracle that her parents would provide a
needy family.

Lori, who lives near Denver, didn't begin to doubt
the reality of Santa until she was about six years old.
Her father, an attorney, would keep her gifts in a safe
in his office. Then, on Christmas Eve, when she was
sleeping, he would bring the presents home and place
them around the tree where Lori would find what
Santa had brought on Christmas morning.

When little Lori would misbehave and need an attitude adjustment, she remembers her mother picking up
the telephone and pretend to talk to Santa Claus, sug-

gesting that he might bypass their home because there was a naughty little girl who lived there.

"I guess this was a Santa Miracle for Mom," Lori joked, "because it really worked on me. I would shift my grumpy attitude immediately and beg her to tell Santa not to skip our house. I would be a good little girl."

Each year, Lori's parents would choose a needy family, and on Christmas Eve would play Santa Claus. "We would all be standing on the doorstep of this family, and when they opened their door to our knocking, they would see us there holding boxes of food, clothing, and toys for the children," Lori said. "I remember smiles, tears, and joy on the faces of those unfortunate families."

Lori said that she will always remember the miracles that her parents brought to those needy families. "Mom and Dad were not dressed up like Santa and Mrs. Claus, but they were playing them in spirit. They were truly enacting the essence of Santa, which is love."

When Jada was six years old, she saw Santa Claus. Since then, she has always considered his appearance some kind of miracle.

"That year, what I really wanted was for Santa to bring me a Christie Barbie doll and leave it under our little Christmas tree. I had been begging my parents all year, but my parents told me that we were living in hard times."

"How can it be hard times for Santa way up in the North Pole?" I would ask my parents. "He must have plenty to eat—why else would he be so fat and jolly?"

That Christmas Eve, young Jada got up to go to the bathroom and heard sounds of laughter coming from the kitchen area.

"I peeked into the kitchen and nearly fell over at the sight my little eyes beheld," Jada said. "Santa Claus himself was just leaving our apartment, and he turned to give Daddy a high-five before he went out the door."

There was no question that it was Santa Claus. Jada saw his bright red cheeks, his long white beard, his red suit lined with white fur, his black boots. It was him.

Jada ran back to bed as fast and as quietly as she could. She knew that if Santa saw her, he just might take back whatever gifts he had left. Kids had to be in bed when he came or he would just leave with his precious bag of goodies.

"I had a really hard time going back to sleep," Jada said. "My little heart was pounding so loud that I was afraid I would wake my sisters Kayla and Ruthie. Ruthie was just a baby, so if she woke up she was likely to start crying—and that would really get me in trouble with both my parents and Santa."

Somehow, Jada recalled, she managed to keep her eyes closed and finally get back to sleep.

"It was really early in the morning when I felt Kayla tugging my arm and telling me that it was time to see what Santa had put under the tree," Jada said. "Ruthie was still asleep, and I motioned to Kayla not to wake her."

It was hard not to start screaming some serious whoops of joy when Jada opened the package with her name on it and found a Christie doll. Kayla got a cloth doll like the kind that their grandmother made for kids. Both the girls agreed that Kayla's doll had come from Santa, though, not from Grandma's sewing basket. Besides, Kayla also got a brush and some stockings.

Later, after her parents got out of bed, Jada proudly displayed her Christie doll. "See," Jada said, "I told you that Santa didn't have any hard times at the North Pole."

She remembers both her parents getting a good laugh out of her economic assessment of conditions outside of the Chicago area. That's when Jada decided to make her confession to her parents.

"I saw you talking to Santa Claus before he left our apartment," Jada said, expecting to get a scolding for sneaking out of bed and violating one of Santa's most sacred rules. "But Mommy and Daddy just smiled, like it was no big deal. I surely had little Kayla's attention though. She was bug-eyed."

Kayla was nearly four, and a firm believer in Santa. "Really?" she asked, her mouth opening wide in total awe. "You really saw Santa with Mommy and Daddy?"

"I suddenly felt endowed and trusted with one of the world's greatest secrets," Jada said. "I was probably one of the few children in the world who had actually seen Santa delivering presents. This wasn't some old fake Santa sitting in a department store. I had seen the real Santa."

"Don't be silly, Jada. You only dreamt you saw Santa," Jada's mom said.

Jada held firmly to her assertion. "I did see Santa, laughing with you and Daddy in the kitchen. Daddy even gave Santa a high-five as Santa left."

Jada thought her father was going to choke with laughter on the piece of toast he was eating. "Well, I know that Santa is one cool cat," he acknowledged. "I would surely like to give the old gent a high-five. I surely would."

In spite of her parents' insistence that she had only been dreaming, Jada persisted in her story, telling every friend, relative, and neighbor that she had really seen Santa Claus on Christmas Eve.

"Now that I am in my mid-forties, I still believe that I saw Santa Claus that night," Jada said. "Somehow, my parents' memories must have been blocked. Maybe they weren't supposed to see Santa, either. Maybe Santa put them in some kind of trance. Who knows?"

Jada has always had what she believes is a solid argument in favor of her really seeing Santa on that magical Christmas Eve. "I clearly saw Santa's red cheeks, his twinkling blue eyes, and all the rest of Santa's features that weren't covered by his white beard," she said. "This was 1968. We lived in the Projects in Chicago. I can't imagine a white man stopping by to visit my parents in the middle of the night unless it really was Santa Claus. And that's why this will always be my Santa Miracle."

Natalie Harrison experienced her Santa Miracle when she was just three-years-old and living with her family in a suburb of Cincinnati.

"My brother Tyler, who was nearly eight, had started in on my parents before Thanksgiving, begging to get a puppy for Christmas," Natalie said. "Since at that time my big brother constituted a large share of my worldview and opinions about nearly every subject, I joined him each night at the dinner table in his perpetual lobbying for a puppy."

Their parents' standard answer was that Tyler was too young to care for a puppy. When Natalie would add her desire for a puppy, she would receive a patronizing chuckle that she was far too young to have a puppy. She could have a puppy doll.

"Tyler is asking for a real, live doggy," her mother would explain. "Not a stuffed toy to have next to you when you sleep. A real live doggy would need to eat and play and go outside to go potty."

Natalie recalled that the argument about going outside to "go potty" would always crack her up. She remembered that she would ask in astonishment why the puppy couldn't use their bathroom like "big girls did." She had just accomplished that major social skill of being potty trained not long before the regular evening discussions about acquiring a dog.

On one occasion, Tyler bribed Natalie with a candy cane to cry at the dinner table that she wanted a puppy for Christmas.

"All that gained me was to be told to stop crying or I wouldn't get any ice cream for dessert," Natalie said. "Then, in a desperate moment of confusion and fear of being deprived a scoop of ice cream, I, for the first and only time in my life, betrayed my big brother. 'Tyler made me say it,' I said, and then really started crying in shame."

Natalie recalled that her father put a hand to his face and exclaimed, "I am absolutely surprised to hear that. I never would have guessed it."

Natalie was too young to understand sarcasm, but she did comprehend that she had cost Tyler his ice cream for dessert.

Natalie was well aware of Tyler saying his prayers at night, kneeling at his bed, asking God, the Baby Jesus, and Santa Claus for a puppy.

"After Mommy had read us a story, she would hear our prayers," Natalie said. "I knew that I pleased Tyler lying in his bed across the room when I also asked the same trinity of sacred figures for a puppy."

Just a week before Christmas, their parents took them to a department story that harbored a Santa Claus in his workshop.

Natalie remembers the layout of Santa Land as a very impressive display. "It was an incredibly awesome place." Tyler, firm in his puppy-quest, marched bravely to the line leading to Santa's Workshop and, when it was his turn, crawled courageously up on Santa's lap and boldly asked for a puppy.

"I wanted to help Tyler in his magnificent effort and add my personal plea to Santa, but as soon as one of Santa's elves set me on the big guy's lap, I screamed bloody murder," Natalie said. "I had seen lots of pictures of Santa. I had seen him on television. On one program he was even dancing with a lot of chorus girls. But facing him in person was just too much. For some reason, Santa just didn't look jolly to me."

Natalie will always remember how Tyler put a comforting arm around her and whispered, "That's all right, Sis. I know you tried."

Christmas Eve brought the Harrison kids a pretty darn nice collection of toys. Among the treasures were a couple of new dolls for Natalie, some G.I. Joe action figures for Tyler, and a number of assorted items to be highly prized. And then there was the underwear that Tyler always got from Aunt Olivia.

But no puppy.

Tyler told Natalie that they still had one more chance. Santa might bring one during the night and leave it under their stockings.

"We were out of bed shortly after sunrise," Natalie said. "Tyler took one of my hands in one of his, put his other hand on the railing, and we went downstairs as quickly as we could."

In their stockings they found candy canes, some new storybooks, and a tiny flashlight for each of them.

Under their stockings was a large stuffed dog.

Natalie looked up at her brother and saw tears forming in his eyes.

"Santa didn't understand me, Nats," Tyler said between sharp intakes of breath, trying desperately to keep from crying. "We wanted a real, live puppy."

At about that very moment, their parents came down the stairs to see what Santa had brought.

"I will always remember Dad walking over and picking up the stuffed dog," Natalie said. "He looked at it with exaggerated puzzlement, turned to Mom, and asked what it was. Mom played right along and said that it must be the dog that the children wanted."

Dad walked around the room, holding the dog under one of his arms. "You know, kids, I think Santa Claus misunderstood you," he said, shaking his head in bewilderment. "Didn't you want a real dog for Christmas?".

Tyler wiped his eyes with a sleeve of his pajamas. "Yes, we did want a real puppy for Christmas." Natalie added her voice to the disappointment, saying, "we wanted a real puppy real bad."

"Well, then," their father said, "it is a good thing that I have been studying magic these past few weeks."

Now it was Natalie's and Tyler's turn to be puzzled.

"Yes," Dad said. "I can turn this stuffed dog into a real puppy by saying a few magic words."

Tyler had shaken off all disbelief and was filled with wonder. "Can you really, Dad?"

At barely three years old, Natalie recalled, she didn't doubt her father's abilities at anything. "If Daddy had said that he could fly, I wouldn't have doubted him for a second."

Their father told them to lie down on the floor under the magical Christmas tree and to close their eyes.

"We heard Dad mumbling abracadabra and a few other magic words," Natalie said, "then I heard Tyler screaming that something was attacking him."

That did it for Natalie. "I opened my eyes and saw Tyler rolling around on the floor with his eyes still shut," she said. "Because his eyes were shut, he couldn't see the puppy that was jumping all over him."

And then Natalie screamed at the top of her lungs. Santa was standing there in the middle of their living room.

"Our neighbor, dressed as Santa, had brought over a puppy for us," Natalie said. "If I had been a little older, I would have recognized Mr. Ellenbecker in the Santa suit and false beard, but at three, it was Santa himself, so I lay on the floor screaming while Tyler at last opened his eyes and began to shout for joy over the puppy that was now tugging on one of his pajama legs with little teeth that we would soon learn were very, very sharp."

Natalie will always consider the jolly old elf's personal delivery of the puppy that they so wanted for Christmas as her greatest Santa Miracle.

"We named the little terrier Bosco," she said, "and he became our friend and defender for many years. Bosco was our living reminder that our father's magic, our prayers, and the miracle of Santa and Christmas can accomplish wonders."

Tuesday Miles, an author and radio host, has observed that in the eyes of a child, seeing is believing and believing is seeing. For one child, however, it was more than merely believing—there really was a Santa Claus; he did have a sleigh; he lived in the North Pole; and in his barn, he had eight very real reindeer.

As Tuesday Miles tells her story:

The date was December 14, 1992. I could smell rain on the horizon, and I had some errands to run. One of them was to drive clear across town to pay a late gas bill so it wouldn't be shut off.

I hated going into this part of town, where you tucked your purse up under your shirt, looking behind you as you walked, fearing someone was about to hit you over the head and steal what little money you had. The only parking was inside a parking garage with five levels of parking. It was dark and cold, and you could hear the sound of your shoes echo as you walked through the garage.

As I finally reached the double glass doors to the office where I had to pay my bill, my eyes were fixated on the ground. I was not a happy camper, having to pay a bill clear across town. My grouchy face announced that I was not in the mood to be nice to anybody even though Christmas was a couple of weeks away.

As I walked across the lobby floor, I raised my eyes, looking up to see where the sound of children's laughter was coming from. I turned the corner, heading toward the counter to pay my bill, and saw a man in a red suit, reading a Christmas story to sixty children in front of him.

It was like an old-fashioned black-and-white movie. My pace slowed and my jaw dropped. I recall saying to myself, *Holy Cow! It can't be. No way. Oh, my God. If there ever was a real Santa Claus, he's right in front of me.*

I was about to stop and listen to the story he was reading when my bill dropped from my hands, reminding me of my errand.

I took a number and sat down in front of the customer service woman. I had already gone over in my head a dozen times what I was going to complain about. I was going to give it to her a piece of my mind.

"Can I help you?" she said.

"I need to pay my bill," I answered. I was also thinking, to myself, *even though I don't have the money and if I paid all of it at once I can kiss my kids' Christmas goodbye.*

The women handed me back my bill and told me to go pay the bill around the corner.

When I got to the front of the line, I braced myself to hear the woman behind the counter say, "You owe $250."

Instead, something odd and unexpected happened. The cashier said to me, "Your total is $35."

A look of shock spread across my face as I asked her if she was certain.

"I am positive," she said. "There was a mistake on your bill. You only owe thirty five dollars."

I knew with no doubt in my mind that I owed an amount of over two hundred dollars. Why all of a sudden did my bill change? Should I speak up and ask again? After all, I did not want to have my gas and water shut off. I turned around and went back to the cashier.

"Are you sure without a doubt that this is correct?"

She took my account number, looked it up, and said, "Yes, this is the amount you owe."

Well, twice was enough. I shut up about it and turned to go back to my car. I started to walk toward another door, hoping to escape from all the children and Santa crowd. When I got to the other doors, they were locked, forcing me to have to walk by the large group. I could hear Santa saying bye-bye to the children and adding a robust, "Merry Christmas to all and to all a good night!"

How cute, I thought to myself.

I walked past them, trying not to make eye contact with anybody. Then I hear this deep, jolly, man's voice say to me, "Merry Christmas young lady!" Not wishing to be impolite, I replied by saying, "Merry Christmas to you also, Santa," and I continued to walk by.

The strangest feeling came over me as I was about to open the two huge doors. I found myself turning around and looking to see if Santa was still standing there.

Yes, he sure was, and he was staring right at me. I let out a sigh and turned around to go say hello to Santa.

"My goodness is your beard real?" I asked.

He nodded yes.

"And your glasses, real?

He nodded yes.

"The tummy all of you?"

"Yep," he replied as he patted his jelly belly.

Then he released a deep and strong, "HO HO HO! That was real, too."

I laughed. How could you not when hearing the sound of jolly ole Saint Nick?

Curious, I began to ask him some questions about his job being Santa each year.

"How much do you charge for special guest appearances?"

"$350 dollars an hour," Santa answered. "I'm booked solid for the rest of the season. People start reserving my services in August."

"Wow!" I exclaimed, impressed by his reputation.

Then I began to tell him about my son who has Cerebral Palsy, mild Autism, and additional intellectual disabilities. I told Santa that for the first five years of his life, my son had a difficult time understanding what the meaning of Christmas was and he barely wanted to open up his presents. Then the year before, he awakened to the Christmas season. I had taken him to go see a Santa and since then, that was all he talked about—Santa this and Santa that. He played Christmas music all year long. My son was in love with Santa.

I soon realized I had taken up enough of Santa's time and I needed to get home. The traffic would start to thicken. I wished him a Merry Christmas and thanked him for all the wonderful smiles he gives children each year. "God bless you," I said, and left.

As I was walking across the cold windy walkway—which always gave me the creeps and is a place where women are not safe to walk alone—I heard footsteps running behind me. I thought to myself, *oh, no please, don't let somebody mug me . . . don't take the little money I have.*

I started to walk faster and faster until I heard this man's voice yell at me, "Miss, Hello? Miss, could you wait for a minute, please?"

It was Santa. Did I forget something?

"I have some extra time Christmas morning," he said when he caught up to me. "I would love to come out and pay a visit to your son and daughter."

I was grateful he asked, but I had to turn him down. "I am so sorry," I apologized. "I would love for you to come. I just can't afford the amount of money you charge for your visits, though I am sure it's worth every penny."

I was just about to turn to leave when Santa grabbed my arm and said, "No, this is my treat. Please, I would love to come visit."

I stood there staring at him, not saying a word. I could not hold my tears. First, the right eye started dripping, then the left.

Santa reached under his sleeve to give me a tissue to wipe my tears, then he reached out and gave me a hug.

"Merry Christmas," he said. "I will see you Christmas morning around eight o'clock. I will bring your children some gifts."

I cried all the way home. I had been blessed twice in one day. The lowered gas bill gave me the extra money I needed for Christmas, and I was able to give my son the gift he had asked for—a visit from Santa. Shaking my head in disbelief as I drove home, I knew I was touched by an angel that day. There was no doubt in my mind that something of a divine order was holding my hand and helping me.

On Christmas morning, both of my kids came into our bedroom, saying that Santa had come and asking if they could open their presents.

After the kids were finished opening the gifts that my husband and I had bought for them, my son walked over to me. "I guess Santa must have forgotten about my wish," he said. "Santa must be busy with all the rest of the kids."

At that moment, the doorbell rang. My son went to see who was at the front door, and right before he opened the door, he heard sleigh bells. He stopped dead in his tracks. He turned to look at me, then ran

for the door yelling, "He didn't forget me . . . it's him
. . . it's him!"

Then the door slowly swung open, and there stood
Santa and Mrs. Claus. Santa had a red velvet bag of
toys slung over his shoulders.

Never in my whole life have I ever seen a kid so
happy. Santa was his hero. He was the man in the big
red suit who flew in his sleigh with eight tiny reindeer
from home to home all around the world. And not just
to children's homes, but to all who wanted to believe
in him.

It never was about the presents. It was always about
this person, Santa Claus, who for one night each year
didn't care about the color of your skin, how much you
had in the bank, whether you were rich or poor. It was
about love—unconditional love.

Nineteen years later, my son's love for Santa has not
changed. He honors him, loves him, demands respect
for him, and waits until Christmas Eve, the night in
which he reunites with his hero each year.

That Christmas morning I took a photo of Santa
and my son. Above their heads, you can clearly see
an amber light glowing. To me, this is the angel who
brought my son his hero, Santa Claus.

When Leigh and her husband adopted their son Wes at six years old, Wes was scared of God and had trouble separating him from the devil. Churches scared him, because they had a ghost inside. He had heard people say so. There was a holy ghost that lived in the churches. He also thought Santa was a bunch of hooey.

Leigh found that there didn't seem to be a clear pathway to teach Wes about God and His trustworthiness and other spiritual lessons. Six-year-old Wes was very cynical about everything. There was no joy in fairy tales or in childhood stories that taught lessons about life. Leigh and her husband had a little curmudgeon on their hands. When she talked about Santa or Christmas, she could just hear him thinking, *Bah! Humbug.*

"So I sat there with little Wes week after week, paying attention to every wish he seemed to make as we watched cartoons or went shopping or any other moment which might present some kind of opening," Leigh said. "Then as if they were reading my mind, the school had a Santa Calling program where a child would get a phone call from Santa a few weeks before the big day."

Leigh had no clue how she would pay for all the things that Wes told Santa that he wanted, but she bought every single thing he asked for. Plus stuff he didn't ask Santa for, but Leigh knew he would love. His uncle bought him a train set, and Leigh's husband sent wonderful gifts from overseas where he was serving in the military. All these gifts would appear for Wes at the big moment.

"But," Leigh said, "the most effective part was this: I took the little guy to grandma and grandpa's house for Christmas. Then we went home."

A true cornucopia of gifts was waiting for Wes when we walked in the door.

"A good friend of ours had sneaked into the house and put all the Santa gifts under the tree," Leigh said. "In addition, there were the gifts that I had wrapped from me and my husband. The tree was hidden by everything. Half the room was packed.

"When Wes walked into the room, he saw that everything was there—everything. And it was just as Mommy had said: Santa had missed him all those years because Santa couldn't find him when he was moving so many times. This year, Santa made sure that Wes got exactly what he wanted because it was the first year that Santa could find him. And Santa always keeps his word."

Leigh explained further to Wes that Santa wasn't God. He couldn't find Wes during those "bad years," but Santa could be trusted.

"That was the beginning," Leigh said. "After that positive experience with Santa, Wes began to give God a second chance. Wes began to flip his values, back to being able to trust."

Maybe Mom was right about some things. He needed to look into the Tooth Fairy and the Easter Bunny, but they all got a second chance.

"Everybody had a second chance, because Wes had finally understood that somebody could be trusted," Leigh concluded. "Thus, little Wes had his second chance! Just what I needed. Just what little Wes needed."

Ray Garcia will always remember the way his mother would sing "Santa Claus is Coming to Town," before Christmas. She would carefully accent the words and make a production number out of the song.

"Mom could easily have been a professional singer," Ray says proudly. "And she did fantastic impressions. I was seven years old in 1968, and, honest to gosh, Mom would do 'To Santa With Love,' in the style of Lulu one night, then, the next, she would be Connie Francis asking 'Where the Elves Are?' She was fantastic as Brenda Lee, 'Rockin' Around the Christmas Tree' and her Streisand version of 'People Who Believe in Santa Are the Luckiest People in the World' was fabulous.

But always, every night, her signature piece was 'Santa Claus Is Coming to Town.'"

It was easy to see why Ray had his own garage rock and roll band when he was eleven, and became a professional musician at seventeen.

"Education was big with Mom," Ray explained, "so I went to college because I promised her that I would. I played a few weekend gigs my first couple of years, but I got a taste of just how hard it would be to make a living as a full-time musician. During my junior year, I began taking education courses, and I became a high school band instructor in 1982."

Ray was so grateful that his mother lived to see him graduate and accept a job with a good-sized high school. "She got cancer when I was a senior in high school," Ray said. "She was a fighter and really did her best to lick the disease, but she died in late August of 1982."

As Ray looks back on his life over a quarter of a century later, he is glad that he was facing the new challenges of teaching music and directing a band in high school to at least partially distract him from his grief.

"I thought of Mom every day," he said, "but if I hadn't been handling the hundred and one daily crises that a high school teacher faces, I undoubtedly would have gone into a deep and total depression. I loved my mother so much."

Ray had a great relationship with his father and his two sisters, but his mother had always been his shining star of inspiration.

"I was such a Mama's boy as a kid," he admitted. "I never stayed overnight at any friend's house until I was in high school. When I was a little kid, I really couldn't bear to be away from Mom. I only liked her cooking, and I avoided restaurants, even hamburger or taco stands, until I started dating."

When Ray graduated from college, he had been seeing someone pretty steadily. "I almost asked her to marry me," he said, "but she was still in college and the high school where I was teaching was more than a hundred miles away, so we decided to see if our love could last the distance. It didn't."

After Thanksgiving, Ray found it impossible not to think about his mother nearly all the time. Again, he was grateful for the multitude of tasks on his plate as the high school bands, choirs, and small musical groups prepared for the annual Christmas program.

"But despite how busy I was with extra rehearsals before and after school, I still found myself missing her. It was, after all, the first Christmas without Mom."

Regardless of what musical piece he was directing, the melody for "Santa Claus Is Coming to Town" kept playing over and over in the echo chamber of his mind.

On occasion, he thought he saw his mother watching him out of the corner of his eye. "This was not a startling or frightening experience," Ray said. "If anything, it was comforting and left me feeling at peace within myself. Mom had been an audience at all my garage band practices. Sometimes, she had delighted the guys by singing along, often doing one of her impressions of some popular singer. All my friends loved her. They all said that I had the neatest mom in all of California. And I always heartily agreed."

At the Christmas concert, the new bandmaster received a standing ovation. Ray was so shocked and surprised at the thunderous approval that he couldn't prevent tears from streaming down his face.

Back at his apartment, Ray poured himself a glass of wine and toasted the photograph of his mother. "We were a success, Mom," he said, tears once again welling in his eyes.

It was at that moment that his elbow bumped the small radio set that he kept in the kitchen. The volume button had been somehow turned on high, and Ray heard, loud and clear, a popular singer's version of "Santa Claus Is Coming to Town."

Ray quickly switched to another station. He didn't need any greater reminder of the loss of his mother that night than to hear her favorite Christmas song blaring out of the radio.

On the next station to which he tuned, he again heard the familiar—the all-too familiar—lyrics of "Santa Claus Is Coming to Town."

As he moved across the dial to all the stations available to his small radio, every station he brought in played the same Christmas song—"Santa Claus Is Coming to Town."

Ray knew that that unique and rather show biz method of communication was his beloved mother's way of telling him that she was with him on this Christmas as she had been on so many others.

Ray knows that not everyone will accept that it was any more than coincidence that station after station was playing the same Christmas song. After all, it was only a few days before Santa really would be coming to town. However, Ray will always believe that it was his mother coming to say "Merry Christmas" and to reach out in a special way to bless him with her love.

Karen recalled the Christmas when she was a senior in high school in 2006. She was inspired by the Assistant Pastor who challenged their Church Youth Group to be creative, bold, imaginative, and come up with some new project to celebrate Christmas by helping others.

"I admit that what I came up with wasn't that new," Karen admitted, "but it had never been practiced in our little city in North Dakota."

In early December, while doing research for a paper on women's voting rights for her sociology class, Karen came across the interesting story of Arianna VanDoorn, assistant to the pastor of Park Congregational Church in Grand Rapids, Michigan, who, in

1908, founded the Santa Claus Girls. Ms. VanDoorn and other Sunday School teachers set out to provide a cheerful Christmas for those unfortunate boys and girls who would not be receiving any gifts from Santa Claus that year. As word spread of the Santa Claus Girls, Senator Arthur H. Vandenberg, editor of the *Grand Rapids Herald*, agreed to sponsor the group so that their funds grew considerably from the few dollars that Ms. VanDoorn's friends had collected. In that first year, more than 150 boys and girls from poor homes received a joyous visit from the Santa Claus Girls.

Karen shared her discovery of Arianna VanDoorn and the Santa Claus Girls with her best friends Lisa and Sandy, who were excited by the idea and agreed with her that it would be wonderful to start their own version of North Dakota Santa Claus Girls in their hometown. They all agreed that their goal would not be to be sponsored by the editor of the local paper or win any support from a state senator, but the three of them could become Santa Claus Girls and help as many poor kids as their limited funds would permit. Among the three of them, they quickly named twenty or so families in their community whose children would be finding empty stockings on Christmas morning.

Karen and Lisa had worked full-time at a fast food restaurant that summer and had been able to set aside quite a nest egg for their college tuition. In addition, they continued to work at the restaurant part-time during the school year. Both of them were willing to contribute a hundred dollars to the cause. Sandy had spent her summer babysitting for her neighbors, so her savings were not as plump as her friends, but she would contribute what she could, maybe fifteen dollars or so.

Karen and Lisa said that since Sandy was an accomplished mistress of the knitting needles, she could compensate by knitting the sides of the cloth Santa Bags that they had assembled from scraps that a fabric store had donated to them. Sandy had knitted matching sweaters for each of them, as well as for her brothers and sisters and her boyfriend, so dressing up some Santa Bags would be a breeze for her. Karen and Lisa freely admitted that they would be more likely to jab themselves with the needles than neatly knit up the sides of the bags.

When other members of the church youth group heard of the project, many of their friends contributed to the cause. Their parents, proud of the unselfish nature of their daughters' project, also donated generously. Within a short period of time, the Santa Claus Girls had collected enough money to be able to put some holiday items and a gift certificate in each Santa Bag.

Since their town was small enough where everyone knew a little bit about everyone else, the Santa Claus Girls were somewhat aware of the needs of the families on their list. In each Santa Bag they placed a bright ornament, some Christmas candy, and a gift certificate to a store where the family could acquire the things they really needed.

On December 21, the Santa Claus Girls set out on their first mission. Their plan was simple and effective. They hung a Santa Bag on the doorknob, rang the bell, or knocked on the door, then ran back into the darkness to await the surprised family member who came to answer the bell. As soon as the Santa Bag was discovered, the three girls shouted, "Merry Christmas from the Santa Claus Girls!" and ran off into the night.

That first night, the girls had distributed nine bags before the temperature turned so cold that they called it a successful initial run and retreated to Lisa's house for some hot chocolate.

December 22 was just too cold to venture out, and their parents forbade their being Santa Claus Girls that night for fear of their being frostbitten.

The next evening, severe cold or not, the girls knew that they simply had to deliver the remaining eleven bags or a lot of poor kids would be liable to receive nothing from Santa Claus that Christmas.

They began their mission just as soon as it grew dark enough to hide their identities and to be able to approach the homes unnoticed. Within a couple of hours, they had delivered eight of the special Santa Bags.

Although Karen said that her nose was as red as Rudolph's because of the cold, she said that she really wanted to deliver the final three bags to three particular families who lived across the city, several blocks away.

Lisa, always a stalwart supporter of any sensible enterprise, declared her friend's goal to be unreasonable—and admitted in no uncertain terms that she was freezing. Sandy nodded in agreement, adding that her toes were frozen. Together, almost as one voice, Lisa and Sandy argued that they could finish the delivery of the last three bags tomorrow night.

Karen reminded them that was Christmas Eve. They would be going to church, and their parents would not want them going out during their own family celebrations after the evening services. Lisa said that there was no way that her father and three brothers would delay Christmas dinner while she was out playing Santa's helper.

"Come on," Karen urged her friends, brushing aside their arguments. "I'll treat if we go into the diner and have some hot chocolate and warm up for a while. Then, if we cut across Schrader's Hill, we can save a lot of walking and time. We'll deliver the last three bags to needy families, and we'll be finished in no time."

The hot chocolate and the warmth of the diner renewed Lisa's and Sandy's enthusiasm to complete their mission, and the three Santa Claus Girls were soon on their way to deliver the last of the Santa Bags and to make some kids have a merrier Christmas.

Schrader's Hill was one of the most popular sledding areas in the city. If it hadn't been so cold that night and getting rather late, the hill would have been crowded with children zipping down the steep hill under the supervision of their parents, many of whom stayed in their cars with the motor and heater running while their kids tromped up and down the slope.

Sandy said that she had never walked across the hill after dark. "I thought they kept the bright lights on all night," she said.

Lisa had read in the local newspaper that the city—in order to conserve on energy and the city budget—would shut off all the lights on Schrader's Hill except for one security light after nine o'clock.

"Be careful," Karen warned. "Some spots are really slippery from all the sleds going up and down the hill."

Sandy had just finished commenting that she had never realized how rough and uneven the hill was when she slipped and took a nasty fall that carried her about twenty feet down the slope before she could come to a stop.

Lisa and Karen ran to help their friend, being careful not to fall on the icy areas of the hill. The moon was mostly covered by clouds, and the single light was now quite some distance away from them. It was very difficult to see the dips, bumps, and the slick spots in the shadows.

They heard Sandy whimpering in pain when they caught up to her.

"I twisted my ankle before I fell," she said. "It really hurts. I don't think I can stand up. Maybe I broke it."

Karen and Lisa tried to support Sandy as she gritted her teeth and tried to stand, but their uneven tugging and pulling on Sandy's coat only made them all fall together on another slick area of the slope.

"Oh, no," Sandy cried. "It feels like my ankle really might be broken. It really, really hurts."

"We have to get help," Karen said. "Lisa, call 911 on your cell phone."

Now Lisa was on the verge of tears. "I was going to do that when we fell," she said. "I dropped the phone. We've got to find it."

Since it had snowed earlier that day, there were several inches of fresh snow in which the cell phone could lie hidden. Karen sighed that there was little chance of finding the phone. Somehow, they would just have to carry Sandy off the hill—and try not to fall too many times doing it.

Things were looking pretty dark for the Santa Claus Girls when who should appear approaching them on a pair of skis but Santa Claus himself.

Santa pulled along beside them and began to speak.

When he could see that they hadn't understood him, he pulled down his beard. "Sorry, I forgot I still had the beard on," he apologized. "What are you three doing out here on such a cold, dark night?"

"Is that you, Jeff?" Lisa asked. "Our senior class vice-president is Santa Claus?"

Jeff agreed that it was indeed he, quickly explaining that his uncle owned the big department store in town and indulged in a bit of nepotism by hiring him to pad himself, put on a beard and a Santa suit, and earn some Christmas spending money by pulling the after-school Santa shift.

"I love to ski," Jeff said, "so I bring my skis to work and ski home across Schrader's Hill. I usually have to be careful not to run into a bunch of kids on sleds."

Sandy said she found all that very fascinating, but she was lying there in the snow in terrible pain. "I think I broke my ankle," she cried.

Jeff called the local ambulance service on his cell phone.

"They will be here in just a few minutes," he assured Sandy. "They said that they were on their way to a Christmas party at the hospital and would be driving right by the hill."

The Santa Claus Girls were stunned when the ambulance pulled up at the base of the hill, and two men dressed in elf costumes got out bearing a stretcher.

"It's a costume party," the paramedics chuckled as they gently placed Sandy on the stretcher. "And you will never guess who's driving—Harriet is dressed up like the Sugar Plum Fairy."

Karen and Lisa knew that Sandy was now in good hands. Jeff called her parents and informed them that she was being taken to the emergency room with either a broken or a sprained ankle.

Harriet, the ambulance driver, asked if she could drop Karen and Lisa anywhere along her route.

Karen explained that they were the Santa Claus Girls, and they had three more stops to make, so if she could just let them off at 400 South Street, they would be very appreciative.

Once Jeff saw that his friends were all right, he disappeared like any good Santa Claus into the night on his skis.

Karen admitted to her friend that she was pretty cold after they had rung the last of the three doorbells and ran into the night.

Lisa shivered in silent response, then moaned, "If only I hadn't lost my cell phone in the snow, I could call my parents to come pick us up."

Karen said that she thought she had an answer to their problem. If they cut across the vacant lot ahead of them and walked two blocks north, they would almost be at Jeff's front door. Since he had appeared out of nowhere and performed one Santa Miracle that night by coming to their rescue, she bet that he wouldn't mind giving the Santa Claus Girls a ride home.

Jeff didn't mind at all. And after he had dropped Lisa off at her home, he had an idea for another holiday surprise when he asked Karen to attend a New Year's Eve party with him.

M arla told us that her husband Chris was the best motorcycle mechanic in North Carolina.

"He has always had a thing about motorcycles and automobiles," she said. "He seems just to have been born with this talent. It is a genuine gift. He can fix anything with a motor. We started dating when we were sophomores in high school, and we got married two years after graduation in 1998."

In spite of his keen mechanical ability, Marla said that Chris has always had a secret ambition to be an actor. Maybe someday a talent scout would come through town, stop at the garage, and discover Chris as the next Marlon Brando, Steve McQueen, or Christian

Bale. He could be an actor and still keep riding bikes, just like Jay Leno and Arnold Schwarzenegger do.

"All of his friends know his little secret fantasy," Marla said, "but they never tease him about his yen for the stage lights, because they respect that this is his hobby. And also maybe because his next favorite hobby is martial arts."

In the summer of 2004, Chris played Captain Hook in the city's Little Theater production of *Peter Pan*. Chris' makeup was so convincing that their six-year-old son Randy didn't recognize his father on stage. When Chris came down into the audience after the play was over, Randy screamed and ran in terror when he approached him.

No way could Marla convince her son that the evil Captain Hook was his very own loving father in disguise, like at Halloween. Only when Chris began to sing "My Heroes Have Always Been Cowboys" did Randy believe that the man on his knees before him was his daddy. (Marla also said that Chris would like to be a country singer.)

At Christmas that year, Chris made a bet with Marla that his skills with makeup were so perfected that he could dress up like Santa Claus and convince Randy that Kris Kringle had paid him an in-person visit.

"I took Chris up on his bet," Marla said. "Mean old Captain Hook was one thing, but sweet, jolly Santa was another. I thought Randy would spot his daddy right away under however much stage makeup he might apply."

Under the pretense that his father had to work late at the garage on Christmas Eve, Randy and Marla began to eat the evening meal.

When a knock sounded at the door, Randy frowned his puzzlement.

"My goodness," Marla said, "who could be coming around at this time of night on Christmas Eve?"

She went to the door, opened it, and cried out in surprise, "Oh, my good gracious, Randy, it is Santa Claus himself."

Marla said that she had to admit that if she didn't know Chris' plan, he might have fooled her as to his identity.

"He had done a terrific job," she said. "The beard, the reddish complexion, the big, plump belly. Everything was perfect."

Without hesitation, Randy crawled up on Santa's lap and received each of the presents from Santa's bag with squeals and giggles of joy.

"Well, Randy, I got to be goin' now," Santa said. "I allowed you to see me in person so that you will know that Santa Claus is real. You earned this privilege because you were a good boy all year long. Now you just keep on listening to your Mommy and Daddy and saying your prayers at night, and I might stop by and see you next year. Right now, I got to get back into my sleigh and visit other good little boys and girls."

Marla said Chris left the kitchen with a dramatic flourish that tempted her to give him a round of applause.

"Well, son, what did you think about that?" Marla said. "You got to see Santa Claus."

By this time, Marla was about ready to concede to Chris that he had won his bet. It surely seemed as though he had convinced Randy that he was Santa Claus.

Randy smiled and said that it was terrific seeing Santa and getting so many terrific presents.

Then, with a twinkle in his eye, Randy added, "And I know Santa Claus is a really cool dude, too. He had a Harley-Davidson motorcycle tattoo on the back of his right hand just where Daddy has one."

Donna told us that she felt fortunate after graduating from a teacher's college in the Midwest in June 2008 when she was able to get a job as an elementary teacher in a small town in California's Central Valley. She was originally a California girl, and her securing a position in the middle of the state would bring her closer to her parents and other family members who lived not far from Fresno. Donna had last visited the almond groves near Newman with her parents when she was twelve or thirteen, and she looked forward to returning to the area as an adult.

September 2008 was an exciting time to begin teaching. The heated election campaigns were drawing to a close, and Donna took great delight in the caliber of the discussions regarding the candidates that her third-grade students exhibited. Donna was amazed at the depth that some of her nine- or ten-year-old students displayed. Some, of course, were parroting comments that they had overheard from their parents, but others seemed genuinely capable of forming surprisingly mature opinions based on their own analyses of media reports.

Donna, as was proper for an elementary-school teacher, remained impartial, nonpartisan beyond criticism. Truly, in college, after she had chosen to teach elementary rather than junior high school or high school, Donna wondered briefly if her idealism to help strengthen children's minds might have been too utopian. But now she realized with each new day that she had made the correct choice. These kids were sharp.

The election results in November brought new topics for discussion after the subjects of reading, writing, and arithmetic were put away for the day. What would happen when the new President would assume office? How thrilling it was to be a part of history with the first African American sitting behind the desk in the Oval Office.

Then, scarcely before one could believe it, it was nearly time for Thanksgiving and Christmas. Because her class contained so many members of diverse ethnic groups, Donna began a series of discussions about the various ways in which Christmas is celebrated in different countries and by different religions.

It was after two or three days of these kinds of discussions that one of the girls asked the single most power-packed question of all. "Is there really a Santa Claus?"

A few of the children giggled, but Donna noticed that suddenly all eyes were fast upon her, as if she were an oracle asked an earth-shaking question that could determine the fate of an entire civilization.

Momentarily puzzled, Donna was intrigued that her bright young nine-year-olds, who had discussed politics and elections with such seeming sophistication, should ask about the reality of Santa Claus.

"Well, I guess that's a question that you should really ask your parents," Donna answered diplomatically, after mentally weighing several possible answers.

Many of the children responded with great determination, not even bothering to raise their hands for permission. Amidst a great deal of confused and rather noisy shouting, the great majority of the class was declaring that Santa Claus was real and would bring them presents that year.

"Quiet, please," Donna said. "Let's remember our manners and courtesy."

"But tell us, please," one of the brightest students in the class asked.

Donna took a deep breath. If these kids could discuss politics and government policies with some apparent depth, they could certainly hear the truth about Santa.

"If you are asking if some chubby fellow in a sleigh drawn by eight reindeers—nine, if you count the one with the red nose—is going to come flying over and drop presents down your chimney, then, no, the answer is that there is no Santa Claus," she told them.

Dismissal bell rang, and Donna gave silent thanks for the classic "saved by the bell."

She felt very uncomfortable as the children filed out of the room in almost total silence. There were no cheery good nights or see-you-tomorrows. On some of those dear cheeks, Donna thought she saw tears.

The next morning before classes began, Donna found a note on her desk from Mrs. Campbell, the principal, requesting that Donna come to her office as soon as she arrived.

Mrs. Campbell, a tall woman who always seemed pleasant, but somewhat severe, asked Donna to sit down opposite her desk.

"I spent a good share of last evening answering telephone calls from very upset parents," she said, getting right to the point. "They were upset and angry because their children came home in tears from your class, crying and feeling in despair because you told them there was no Santa Claus."

Donna almost made the mistake of assuming that Mrs. Campbell was joking, but when she considered the tone of her voice, she concluded that she was quite serious.

"One of the reasons that you were hired," Mrs. Campbell explained, "was because of your high academic standards. Some of your professors even wrote on their recommendations that you were one of those students who always had her nose in a book."

Donna began to acknowledge such praise, but Mrs. Campbell held up her hand to silence her.

"The world of academics is often a world apart from the real world," Mrs. Campbell said. "A good teacher has to learn to straddle both."

Mrs. Campbell went on to explain that in the five years that Donna had been away obtaining her master's degree in education in the Midwest, the Central Valley had undergone three years of serious drought. In 2009, the coming year, the University of California had estimated that the drought may cause

847,000 acres to go unplanted and that there may be a loss of 70,000 jobs.

"From your visits to Central Valley in your childhood, you remember it as one of the richest farming regions in the nation," Mrs. Campbell said. "Because of the drought, many of your students' parents are broke, terribly in debt. Christmas is soon approaching. The children need Santa Claus. They need the miracle of hope. With their last pennies, these wonderful people will see that Santa Claus will come for their children. Their children will have a Christmas."

Mrs. Campbell paused to remove a book from a desk drawer. She explained that she was from New York originally, and she had always loved Betty Smith's famous novel, A *Tree Grows in Brooklyn*. In the book, Mrs. Campbell said, among her favorite passages are those in which a grandmother explains to her daughter, a young mother, why a child must be taught to believe in Santa Claus—even if the mother herself may not believe.

Mrs. Campbell asked Donna's indulgence to allow her to read a few paragraphs in which the grandmother says that a child must start out in life believing in things not of this world: "Then when the world becomes too ugly for living in, the child can reach back and live in her imagination."

Mrs. Campbell said that she would be retiring in another two years. "As a teacher, I have witnessed miracles among the children," she said. "Only by remembering these miracles in my mind can I live beyond what I have to live for."

Donna walked to her classroom in silence. One day the children would be able to decide for themselves about Santa Claus. Now it was important that they should believe with all their hearts in the true miracle of Santa.

"Good morning, class," she greeted the children seated before her. "I think I have some explaining to do. Yesterday, when you asked about Santa Claus, it was just time for dismissal, and I guess we all got excited and started talking at once. Now, about Santa Claus, what I meant to explain was that those men in department stories with pillows stuffed under their red suits were not the real Santa. Of course those men, nice as they may be, are not able to fly across the sky in a magic sleigh and bring presents to your homes.

"Now then, about the *real* Santa Claus," Donna smiled, "he lives in all of our hearts and knows everything that we want for Christmas. Don't ask me how he does it. It is just a miracle that Santa Claus is able to work."

The smiles and tears of joy and relief that shone from the children's faces provided Donna with her own Santa Miracle that she knew would last her a lifetime.

Annette Martin has become world famous as a psychic counselor and a professional singer. She is the subject of the book *Gift of the White Light: The Strange and Wonderful Story of Annette Martin* by James N. Frey.

Here is Annette's story of how she received her Santa Miracle:

When I was ten years old, my family moved to a house situated in the middle of the block in the Sunset District of San Francisco, just a few blocks from the Pacific Ocean. My back bedroom window looked out to the vast ocean, and when I opened it, I could smell the luscious salt air.

St. Gabriel's Grammar school on 38th Avenue was eight blocks toward the ocean. On sunny days I would walk to, and back from, school. On cold, foggy, and rainy days, I would hop onto the L Street car that ran up and down Taraval Street, with its metal wheels churning along the tracks.

After about two months or so, new friends were beginning to come into my life, but most of them still kept themselves an arm's length away. My singing had come into full blossom, and our principal, Sister Mary Hillary, asked me to sing in the adult choir due to my voice being so powerful at such a young age.

My singing was becoming very popular, and I was asked to do a TV show with Del Courtney at KPIX. I was studying voice, and I felt that this would be a great opportunity to sing even more. The only trouble was that my school friends began to back away even farther and not even be as superficially friendly as they were before.

As the days went by, a sadness came into my life and I felt very alone. Sure, I had my music and could see things that others could not, but something was missing.

About a month later my folks drove down to Palo Alto onto the Stanford University property. Mother had found one of her old teachers from Commerce High in San Francisco and had been invited for lunch.

We walked in and were greeted by the most beautiful thing I had ever seen—a long-haired golden retriever. I went to my knees and just started to cry. I was enveloped by this incredible creature. She was so soft and loving, and she seemed to want to be with me the entire time that we were there visiting.

When it was time to leave, I felt so sad, and I wished that I could take her home with me. Mom and Dad were quite surprised by my response to the retriever, as I had never been around dogs my entire life. I had only been exposed to one animal—Fifi, my grandmother's Persian cat.

Life went on. I continued with all of my school and professional singing engagements, but as an only child, my days were becoming more lonely. No friends to speak of and only adults that really didn't want to carry on lengthy conversations with a ten-year-old. I had such a longing to have a friend or companion. I went to church many days, asking for that special miracle . . . but nothing seemed to be happening.

December rolled around, and it was soon Christmas Eve. My grandparents were coming over for Christmas morning breakfast and the opening of gifts.

The morning arrived, and after breakfast my daddy went down to the basement and told me to close my eyes, as I was going to be the first to open packages. Keeping my eyes tightly shut and anticipating great excitement over what Santa may have brought me, Daddy said, "Okay, honey, open your eyes."

Slowly, opening first one eye and then the other, I could see a big basket in front of the tall, white-flocked Christmas tree. Moving toward the basket, I could hear something inside, and I rushed to open the lid. A little cry came from the basket, and I peered inside to discover a golden fluff looking up at me with big brown eyes.

I screamed for joy and reached in and grabbed this adorable puppy and just cried and cried, "Thank you, Daddy and Mommy. Thank you, Santa," over and over again.

My prayers had been answered. Now I had a companion with whom to play and to tell all of my inner secrets.

I named her "Rochanne," a combination of our last name, De La Roche, and Anne, being part of my first name.

Rochanne, my Santa Miracle, lived to be fifteen years old and bore ten of the most precious puppies on my bed. The memory of my dear companion still brings tears to my eyes when I think of her.